"Are you — or is someone you know — discerning a call to the priesthood? *All In: Breaking Barriers to Discerning the Priesthood* is a fabulous book that will help you on your journey. Isacco and Tirabassi identify various psychological obstacles young men face today and offer practical steps to turn those barriers into bridges, moving forward. As a mother of sons actively discerning, I highly recommend this book!"
— **Kimberly Hahn, Author of** *Life-Giving Love: Embracing God's Beautiful Design for Marriage*

"I've never seen a more practical and pastoral guide to discerning a vocation to the priesthood. This book is going to change a lot of lives."
— **Matthew Leonard, Vice President, St. Paul Center for Biblical Theology**

"Isacco and Tirabassi simplify discernment in this concise, candid, and practical approach ..."
— **Fr. Michael R. Ackerman, Director of Priestly Vocations, Diocese of Pittsburgh**

"I wholeheartedly recommend the book ... as an encouragement to those men who are meant to "dream, set big goals, and to explore the wonders of uncertainty" ... through discerning the call to priesthood."
— **Dr. Christina Lynch, Director of Psychological Services, St. John Vianney Theological Seminary**

D1248568

CPSIA information can be obtained
at www.ICGtesting.com
Printed in the USA
BVHW04s2349121018
529488BV00009B/9/P

ALL IN

ALL IN

BREAKING BARRIERS TO DISCERNING THE PRIESTHOOD

ANTHONY ISACCO, PH.D
DOMENICK TIRABASSI, M.S.

LAMBING PRESS I PITTSBURGH

Lambing Press

Copyright © 2018 Anthony Isacco, Ph.D

Domenick Tirabassi, M.S.

Imprimatur: Most Rev. David. A. Zubik

Bishop of Pittsburgh

The *Imprimatur* is a declaration that a book is considered to be free from doctrinal or moral error. It is not necessarily implied that those who have granted them agree with the contents, opinions or statements expressed.

Published in the United States by Lambing Press.

www.LambingPress.com

ISBN 978-0-9978215-6-7

Book design by Christina Aquilina

Anthony: To the Saint Paul Seminary Community

(Pittsburgh, PA)

Domenick: To Saint Francis de Sales Seminary

(Milwaukee, WI) &

Saint Joseph College Seminary (Chicago, IL)

TABLE OF CONTENTS

FOREWORD

By Fr. Joseph Freedy

"The world offers you comfort, but you were not made for comfort. You were made for greatness."
– Pope Benedict XVI

The desire to do something great with our lives burns within each one of us. Mel Gibson's 2016 film *Hacksaw Ridge* ignited this desire for greatness within me when I went to see it in the theater. The film traces the incredible true story of Desmond Doss, a medic in WWII who saved the lives of seventy-five men over the course of one night without firing a rifle. During battle, Doss knelt by the body of a friend who had just been killed, unsure of what to do amidst the chaos raging around him. He desperately prayed to God, "What is it you want of me? I don't understand. I can't hear You." An explosion blasted nearby, and from it, Doss heard someone call, "Medic!" Immediately, Doss understood God's will and acted. He rushed to the heart of the explosion, pulled the man to the edge of Hacksaw Ridge, and lowered him over to safety. Exhausted, Doss prayed, "Please Lord, help me get one more." He prayed this prayer all through the night as he saved the lives of his fellow soldiers.

After watching *Hacksaw Ridge*, I felt inspired to be all that God is calling me to be: a great man, a great priest, and ultimately, a great saint. Though I am far from attaining such greatness, this movie reminded me that we are all searching for heroic virtue or sanctity. We strive for this sanctity through God's perfect plan for our lives: our vocation. Our vocation fulfills our desire to commit our lives to something worth the complete gift of ourselves.

Choosing between the two incredible vocations of marriage and the priesthood seems an impossible choice indeed. Yet true discernment is not about choosing; it is about following. The first step in discernment is to decide to follow, and then when the path is indicated, to take that path. Discernment is a wholehearted *yes* to following, and then a *yes* again to a particular path. Doss first said *yes* to follow the Lord and clung unwaveringly to his beliefs. When he heard the cry, "Medic!" he recognized it as God's voice and knew exactly where God was calling him. As a result of Doss's *yes*, the lives of seventy-five men were saved that night.

This wholehearted *yes* to following Jesus echoes in the pages of the Scriptures through the Call of Matthew. We have heard this story so many times that we often miss its drama. Jesus approached Matthew working at the customs post and said, "Follow me." The next verse shows how intensely Matthew was affected by this brief encounter with Jesus: "And [Matthew] got up and followed Him" (Mt. 9:9). Why did Matthew follow Jesus so quickly, so readily, leaving behind the security of the life he knew? Jesus offered Matthew a fullness of life that Matthew had never before experienced. Something in Jesus corresponded to the deepest longings of Matthew's heart. When Matthew looked into Jesus's eyes, he must have experienced the love for which he knew he was made.

Matthew stayed in the gaze of Jesus, a gaze that the rich young man missed (Mk. 10:17-22). After the rich young man told Jesus that he had observed all the commandments as Jesus prescribed, the Gospel of Mark describes Jesus's response: "Jesus, looking at him, loved him and said to him, 'You are lacking in one thing. Go, sell what you have, and give to [the] poor and you will have treasure in heaven; then come, follow me'" (Mk. 10:21). I am convinced that the rich young man turned away sadly because he missed the gaze of Jesus. If he had allowed himself to be caught up in the love, the fulfillment, the sense of belonging that Jesus freely offered in that gaze, he never would have left Him.

Jesus clearly and lovingly invited both Matthew and the rich young man to follow Him. The rich young man could not raise his eyes from his possessions, but Matthew did not miss the piercing gaze of Jesus, inviting him to adventure and fulfillment. Matthew knew that his heart's deepest longings would be completely satisfied in that gaze. The Lord wants to do the same for us. He wants us to remain in the loving gaze that He offers us at every moment of our lives, and there, decide to follow Him. Once we make this decision, He will reveal in His time the path, the vocation, through which He desires us to strive for sanctity.

In this book, Dr. Anthony Isacco and Domenick Tirabassi, M.S. offer practical advice that will help men discern a call to the priesthood. Isacco and Tirabassi identify and dismantle common psychological barriers that impede men from freely discerning this vocation. They also offer concrete advice on how to take a simple and active approach to the discernment process. Their extensive backgrounds in psychology give them the expertise to address these issues.

People often needlessly complicate the discernment process. Isacco and Tirabassi identify the psychological barriers that lead to these complications. They offer a realistic view of marriage and present a countercultural, yet poignant portrait of masculinity that aligns with the Catholic faith. They also explain how to face personal insecurities and social pressures that impede authentic discernment. Bringing the book to conclusion, Isacco and Tirabassi detail the active discernment steps that men can take. They describe the humility required to reexamine one's discernment process and the courage necessary to follow the path God reveals.

When Desmond Doss was faced with the choice of heeding the call for a medic, he did not hesitate; he acted. He feared for his life, but nonetheless, he followed the call. For Doss, discernment seemed rather simple: he asked God what He wanted of him, heard the cry, and rushed to aid the wounded man. Often, discernment proves much more complicated, or we make it so ourselves. This book strives to simplify discernment so that discerners can hear God's call and follow it with great generosity. The foundation of all discernment must be a deep and steadfast trust that God knows well the plans He has for us (Jer. 29:11), and that following these plans will lead to our greatest happiness.

May God bless you on your journey.
Father Joseph Freedy

CHAPTER 1

I N T R O D U C T I O N

What do you want to be when you grow up? If you think back to your childhood, you can probably remember being asked the "career question" by family, friends, and teachers. People are asked the "career question" hundreds of times throughout their childhood and adolescence. Most children are full of enthusiasm when they describe their dreams of becoming a professional basketball player, an astronaut, the President of the United States, or a Jedi Knight. Indeed, childhood is a time to dream big. We have tried moving objects with our minds. Unfortunately, the Force does not work like it does in the movies.

By the time adolescence strikes, some of the glimmer and enthusiasm of our younger years wanes. Our minds often shift toward more practical careers. As young adults, our attention turns from President to accountant, Jedi Knight to engineer, and from professional basketball player to lawyer. When we think we finally have it figured out, life happens. The world is quick to help us fall back into questioning whether we picked the right career. Let's fill you in on a little secret: figuring out what you want to do with your life is bigger than picking a career. We are meant to dream, to set big goals, and to explore the wonders of uncertainty. Our exploration is supposed to go beyond discovering what will provide us with money to pay the bills.

This idea is not new. In the early 1900s, a man named Frank Parsons helped immigrants in the United States find work. His passion led to the establishment of the first Vocational Bureau in 1908, and his influential work, *On Choosing a Vocation*, was published in 1909. The title of the book does not contain the word *career* or *job* but *vocation*. Parsons always believed that choosing a vocation meant much more than picking a job. A job pays the bills in exchange for a service that you provide. Someone with a job may say, "I work from 9 to 5. I clock in and clock out." That is the essence of paid employment. On the other hand, a *vocation* is something much deeper. It requires reflecting on your interests, strengths, values, and abilities. A vocation is intended to provide purpose and meaning to your life. Someone who lives his vocation may say, "I enjoy what I do so much, I have never really *worked* a day in my life."

Vocation has special meaning in the Catholic Church. Catholics believe that God plays a key role in helping people think about, identify, and commit to their vocation (USCCB, 2017). Choosing a vocation does not just include considering what *you* want to do, but also what *God* wants you to do. We believe that people find ultimate happiness and purpose in their lives when they commit to a vocation that integrates both their desires and God's desires for them. Matching our desires with God's desires for us is ideal, but it can be extremely challenging as well. There are thousands of examples of people who, upon learning of God's desires for them, have replied with a "thanks but no thanks." The "thanks but no thanks" impulse occurs in most men when the idea of the priesthood slowly enters their minds. Whether they hear this calling in prayer, or someone from church says, "I think you would make a great priest," they often respond with a resounding "No way!"

WHAT IS A CATHOLIC PRIEST?

A Catholic priest is an ordained minister within the Catholic Church. Catholic priests administer the sacraments, run parishes, and are responsible for the spiritual life of their parishioners. This basic description is something you might find in a Religion 101 textbook. Yet, priests are so much more. Their role in the Catholic Church and people's lives is almost beyond description.

Priests represent God to the people. They become intimately involved in people's lives at their highest and lowest points in life. Priests are present in experiences of deep despair and grief like funerals and celebrate the most joyous occasions like weddings and baptisms. As Pope Francis says, a priest is meant to get his hands dirty while working closely with people in the messiness of their lives. Of course, dirty is not meant literally but metaphorically to emphasize the intimate, difficult, and indispensable relationship between priests and people. Try to imagine the immense responsibility and awesomeness that comes with being a priest.

The life of a priest offers such a wide array of powerful experiences that some or all of these aspects must seem appealing to you. You may have thought of a priest from your life who has made a lasting and positive impact on you. Some part of you may be thinking of becoming a priest as well. If you are thinking of becoming a priest, our simple response is give it a try. We recognize that it is too simple of a response. We have helped numerous men decide what they want to pursue with their lives. It is a complicated, tough decision. The reality is that there are so many reasons not to be a priest.

DON'T DO IT!

For all the amazing life experiences that come with being a priest, there are many reasons not to be a priest. Let's identify some of the more common reasons why you may say to yourself, "Yeah, the priesthood is great and all, but not for me."

First, Catholic priests don't make a lot of money. In our culture, people often view money as a sign of power, respect, and success. Men are usually expected to be providers, and men who fail to provide for others can be viewed as lazy, unsuccessful, or less valuable. A common phrase is, "Here is the *real* Golden Rule. . . the one with the gold makes the rules." The point is well known and well taken. Money brings power, prestige, and respect, which almost everyone desires on a basic level. You'll learn this message a lot throughout the book—the priesthood is very countercultural. Priests are definitely countercultural when it comes to money.

Priests who belong to a religious order such as the Jesuits, Franciscans, or Servants of the Christ Jesus take a vow of poverty. A vow of poverty is pretty significant. Let's look at one example. The Servants of the Christ Jesus are a new religious order of priests in Denver, Colorado. They keep two to three uniforms for their clothing, two pairs of sandals, and budget $1 per person, per meal. Yes, $1 per meal sounds impossible. On the other hand, diocesan priests aren't part of a religious order; you typically encounter them at your local parish. Diocesan priests don't take a vow of poverty but are expected to live a simple life. A promise of simplicity means that a diocesan priest can still buy a smartphone and have other possessions. Each diocesan priest has the freedom to live as simply as he chooses.

For example, St. John Paul the Great was a diocesan priest in Poland before becoming pope. In the pope's biography, George Weigel describes St. John Paul's early years as a young parish priest in Poland. According to Weigel, St. John Paul could fit all his possessions in one suitcase, which he took with him when he was transferred from parish to parish. All of your possessions in one suitcase is pretty extreme. Of course, not all priests live as simply as St. John Paul. We have helped a few priests move and can say that some priests have a lot of stuff, just like everyone else. Some diocesan priests have a boat or season tickets to their favorite sports team. Here is the point—if you are looking for a life and career full of money and power, the priesthood does not make sense, but its life of simplicity may not be as extreme as you may think.

Second, these days Catholic priests don't get the respect or hold the high social status that they used to. Ask your parents, grandparents, or great-grandparents about how people viewed priests when they were younger. You may hear stories about the mythical "Fr. Patrick" from their parish years ago, who ruled the parish like a prince, dispensed wise advice that was never questioned and always followed, and caused grown men to straighten their ties in his presence.

Perhaps nobody embodied the old-school image of a priest during that time than Archbishop Fulton Sheen. If you have not heard of him before, a quick Google search can fill in some blanks for you. Think about this: Archbishop Sheen had a primetime television show called *Life Is Worth Living* on a major network from 1951 to 1957. The show won Emmy Awards and drew an estimated ten million viewers per week. With those ratings during the 2016–2017 year, *Life Is Worth Living* would have been a top-10 show, on par with viewership for *The Voice*, *Dancing with the Stars*, and *NCIS: Los Angeles.* It's hard to imagine a priest enjoying such a prestigious role in today's society and culture.

Of course, the image of the priesthood has taken a hit over the past fifteen years due to the sexual abuse scandal. There is no excuse for the sexual abuse of minors and hierarchical coverups. Some priests and bishops deserve all the negative attention they get. This book is not about the sexual abuse scandal, but we recognize the enormous and perhaps incalculable impact it has had on the victims, the Catholic Church, priests, the rank-and-file Catholics. We know friends and family members who have distanced themselves from the Catholic Church after the sexual abuse scandal. It makes sense that men don't want to become priests because of the negative media attention, a stereotype of all priests as pedophiles, and fears of backlash from family and friends.

Compounding that negative image of the priesthood is the nearly constant reminder that we, as Catholics, need to pray for more men to become priests because there is a priest shortage in the United States. The priest shortage is a reality. From 1985 to 2016, the total number of priests decreased from 57,000 to 37,000 (CARA, 2017). The total number of seminarians in 2016 was 3,520, down from 4,063 in 1985 (CARA, 2017). We understand that it's a tough "sell" to ask a man to consider joining a religious group that has been associated with criminal behavior and discussed as if they are an endangered species, on the verge of irrelevance. Nobody wants to join a losing team. Think of NBA superstar Kevin Durant. In 2016, he left his home team, the Oklahoma City Thunder as a free agent and signed with the Golden State Warriors. The Warriors had just lost game 7 of the NBA championship but won the league championship the previous year and were stacked with talented players. The Warriors, with Kevin Durant, won the 2017 championship. In short, Kevin Durant signed with the team that gave him the best opportunity to win a championship. He didn't sign with the worst team in the NBA because he wanted to be a winner. We are all like Kevin Durant in the sense that we want to belong to a winning team.

In some ways, many people misperceive the Catholic Church in a way that mirrors the negative perception of priests. We have heard people describe the Catholic Church as a bunch of elderly women in the pews governed by a bunch of elderly men in the hierarchy. Many Church teachings are considered out of touch with modern, secular society. And we have talked with young men who have openly questioned if they would be spending their lives as priests drinking coffee with a few elderly women after the morning rosary group. It is understandable if you ask yourself, "Where is the action, excitement, and risk in the priesthood?" Priests save souls but usually not by running into burning buildings or by pulling a hurt driver from a car wreck. Indeed, the way priests save souls is just as dramatic, but these rescues are much quieter and don't make headlines.

Third, many people perceive the priesthood as boring, repetitive, no fun, and consisting of too many rules: for example, Catholic priests do not get married and are not allowed to have sex. For any typical, red-blooded American man, those rules can be a real bummer. We recently spoke to young men at a couple of Catholic high schools about their careers, lives, hopes, and dreams. We asked the young high school men how many of them wanted to get married and have a family. Just about 100% of those young men raised their hands. Even if we account for the social pressure to raise your hand in front of your friends and classmates, we can safely say that most young men envision their future with marriage, children, and a career. Marriage is both a standard and noble vision in its own right. The world and the Church need great Catholic fathers that form joyful, vibrant Catholic families. Indeed, marriage is one of the primary vocations promoted by the Catholic Church.

And finally, you may have a hard time seeing yourself as a priest because you are having a hard time seeing yourself as a Catholic or even particularly religious. According to the

PEW Research Center, the number of Catholics decreased by 3% between 2007 and 2014 while the religiously unaffiliated increased by 7%. Many people describe themselves as "spiritual but not religious." We can all name several people in our lives who aren't practicing Catholics anymore. There are many reasons why people have disconnected from the Catholic Church, too many to list here. The point is that it is very difficult to consider the priesthood seriously if you have major doubts about the Church in which priests live and work.

Let's recap. We are asking you to rethink the possibility of the priesthood. Yet, we recognize the many barriers that may be in your way. As a priest, you won't have a lot of money, you won't get married, and you won't have sex. You might perceive life as a priest to be boring or be afraid that people will associate you with pedophiles. Frankly, you might not even want to be Catholic anymore. Without a doubt, that is a tough list. It is difficult to decide whether to laugh or cry about it.

WELCOME BACK, GOOD MEN

In 2002, Michael Rose wrote *Goodbye, Good Men*, a compelling and controversial book that details the mass exodus of men from seminaries. His central thesis, sixteen years ago, was that conservative men were pushed out of seminaries by a liberal agenda. Mr. Rose offered one way to explain the priest shortage: a political reason. In contrast, our central thesis is not political but psychological. We argue that God has not stopped calling good men to the priesthood, but that men encounter an array of barriers that previous generations did not. In this book, we identify and debunk *psychological* barriers.

Spirituality and psychology are closely linked. As you might know, the word "psychology" comes from the Greek *psyche* (soul) and *-logy* (the study of). Many early psychologists who were committed to this "study of the soul" didn't shy away from making comments about religion or spirituality. We continue this tradition of belief that our spirituality and psychology are deeply intertwined. As a result, you can greatly benefit from understanding more about the way psychology might be at play in your thoughts and feelings about choosing your vocation and, possibly, the priesthood.

When we talk about psychological barriers, we are referring to thoughts, ideas, or concerns that prevent men from clearly discerning the priesthood in a simple and active way. These barriers stop men from responding to God's call by clogging their thoughts with unrealistic, fearful, and illogical clutter. By debunking the barriers and providing a path for committing to God's plan, we hope that this book is a "Welcome Back" sign to good men discerning the priesthood.

GOING *ALL IN*

As psychologists, professional counselors, and Catholic men, we have firsthand experience working with men who have run into obstacles on their path to the priesthood. Whether you are a high schooler who has dabbled with the idea of becoming a priest, or a transitional deacon who is having some reservations about priestly ordination, we hope this book can help you find clarity in your discovery of God's will in your life. We have learned that many men face similar barriers. They have similar concerns and questions that make discernment more challenging. What will my friends and family think? Am I holy enough to be a priest? Could I ever live as a celibate man? Is now the right time to enter the seminary? Maybe I should wait longer? Maybe I should date more?

This book directly addresses those concerns and questions. In turn, we provide you with insight, reflections, and activities that help you to answer God's call.

✣ **CHAPTER 2** sets the stage for your active discernment by explaining the psychology of action. Action enables you to overcome the common psychological barriers, which we discuss in Chapters 3–8.

✣ **CHAPTER 3** challenges the barrier that discernment has to be a long, agonizing journey. Men who are stopped by this barrier are often described as "perpetual discerners."

✣ **CHAPTER 4** helps men to look beyond their need to know with absolute certainty that God is calling them to the priesthood. Men become stuck in their discernment due to an irrational need to know with 100% absolute, iron-clad certainty that God is calling them to be priests.

✣ **CHAPTER 5** overcomes the barriers created by unhelpful views of masculinity, which prevent men from embracing priesthood.

✣ **CHAPTER 6** explains how discouragement from parents, friends, and family may prevent men from discerning the priesthood clearly, while encouragement from family and friends can promote a vocation.

✣ **CHAPTER 7** breaks down the barrier caused by men's sense of unworthiness, which can distort discernment with shame. We often hear men say, "I am not worthy enough to be a priest" and so don't move forward with their discernment.

✣ **CHAPTER 8** breaks down the barrier created by an unrealistic fantasy of dating and marriage that can confuse men and detour men in their discernment.

✟ **CHAPTERS 3–8** not only identify and describe the common barriers, but also debunk the psychological barriers and give you practical steps to simplify the discernment process.

✟ **CHAPTER 9** helps you to identify your strengths and how they can serve the Church.

✟ **CHAPTER 10** encourages you to stop reading and start going *All In* with your discernment.

At the end of each chapter, we will provide you with *Simple and Active* steps that will guide you in your discernment process.

CHAPTER 2

THE PSYCHOLOGY OF ACTION

Pope Francis recently told priests, "For the flock he is a shepherd, not an inspector, and he devotes himself to the mission not fifty or sixty percent, but with all he has." Pope Francis wants men to give it their all. That is what we are asking you to do—give *your all* to discernment through actions that break down barriers and open you to learning God's plan for your life. We believe that discernment isn't meant to be passive, but active. If you approach your discernment with the mentality that you can just sit back and wait for something to happen, then we bet that you'll be waiting for a very long time.

Despite the clear benefits of active discernment, men often hesitate and stay passive. The Church needs men to say yes to the priesthood despite the barriers identified in Chapter 1. In fact, the Church needs men to become priests because of those barriers. You cannot stand by passively and let the barriers immobilize you. You'll miss engaging in activities, opportunities, and experiences that will help you grow, discover your vocation, and find more meaning in your life. We encourage you to be active throughout this book. Let's further explain the active mentality that we hope you embrace.

JUMP INTO THE SWIMMING POOL

In 2011, Archbishop Listecki was invited to speak at a

retreat for men who were thinking about the priesthood. He recognized that many men struggle with the idea of becoming a priest and can easily fall into inaction. The archbishop offered some advice to these men, who may have been sitting on the fence. The archbishop turned to the group of men and said, "If you want to know whether or not you like to swim, you have to get in the pool." He paused for a moment to let his words sink in, then repeated them, "If you want to know whether or not you like to swim, you have to get in the pool!" After a few seconds, it became clear that Archbishop Listecki was talking about the priesthood and seminary. He went on to explain one of the best ways to know if God is calling you to be a priest is by discerning the priesthood from within the walls of the seminary.

He continued his metaphor and elaborated on how each person might have a different approach to getting in the pool. Some people cannonball right into the deep end. They hear the call of God, join the seminary, and never turn back. Others prefer to dip their toes in the water, check the temperature, then take the stairs into the pool. They hear the call of God, explore, and ease their way into seminary. Regardless of the initial approach, the archbishop's point stands: "If you want to know whether or not you like to swim, you have to get in the pool!"

The metaphor speaks to the value of being decisive, taking tangible steps to figure out God's will in your life, and learning from these new experiences. We agree with the archbishop: the best way to know if you're called to the priesthood is to engage in behaviors and activities that are about the priesthood. When we were thinking about becoming psychologists, we took psychology classes, talked to other psychologists, and researched psychology programs. It would have been strange if we were thinking about becoming psychologists and avoided psychologists, took classes in accounting, and applied to law school.

THE PSYCHOLOGY OF JUMPING INTO THE POOL

We did our due diligence to write this book. We reviewed a lot of other books, articles, and websites about discerning a vocation. And we talked to many priests, seminarians, vocation directors, parents, and young men. In all our research and discussions, we discovered collective wisdom aimed to help men discern their vocation through actionable steps. Those steps all started with prayer. It is impossible to hear and respond to a call from God without a relationship with God that is rooted in prayer. Prayer comes first. It puts you in the right frame of mind to take action. Prayer also opens a direct line of communication with God, inviting him into your experiences and enabling you to call on him for support.

The people we spoke with gave us several activities that can promote the discernment process. After highlighting the importance of "prayer first," they advised young men to:

- ✝ Join a men's discernment group
- ✝ Attend a vocations discernment retreat
- ✝ Talk with a vocation director
- ✝ Visit a seminary
- ✝ Speak with current priests and seminarians
- ✝ Spend a day shadowing a priest

All these actions can typically be done within your local diocese. They are usually free and require minimal work to set up, such as making a short phone call or a few clicks on the Internet. Thinking back to the archbishop's metaphor, all of these activities get you into the swimming pool. They are akin to dipping your toes in from the side or wading in the shallow end of the pool, which gives you a feel for the water.

The activities we mentioned serve several other important purposes. First, you may learn that the priesthood is not for you and you can rule it out. Ruling out through experience is better than ruling out without ever trying. Let's consider, as an example, a parent who is introducing new food to their child. The father makes sunny-side up eggs one Saturday morning instead of the usual scrambled eggs. He places the hot, delicious, protein-packed eggs in front of his child for breakfast. The child then disgustedly asks, before ever taking a bite, "What is that?!" as if the parent is serving poison on a platter. The child quickly declares, "I am NOT eating that!!" rejecting the sunny-side up eggs before giving them a chance. Contrast this example with a child who is given the eggs, takes a bite, and realizes he does not like the taste. The child then tells his father, "Dad, I'm not a big fan of these eggs. Let's stick to cereal in the future." The second child made a mature and informed decision based on his experiences. The same can be said about discerning a vocation. Your experiences can help you to rule out the priesthood in a mature and well-informed way.

Second, talking to current seminarians, observing the daily work of priests, and visiting the seminary can help demystify the whole preconceived image of what it is like to be a priest. Many men think being a priest entails praying in isolation or sitting around drinking coffee with elderly people all day. We have heard young men describe a seminary as a kind of medieval castle with long, dark hallways and seminarians walking to and fro with torches at night. Those preconceived notions are outdated stereotypes.

Most men are pleasantly surprised to learn that seminary buildings are modern, bright, welcoming places with computers, classrooms, workout facilities, a chapel, electricity, and indoor plumbing. Many seminaries are located on beautiful campuses, perfect for walking, contemplation, and appreciating God as the Creator of nature. Shadowing a priest provides insight into the unique and multifaceted ways that a priest lives out his ministry through visiting hospitals, hearing confessions, saying mass, or even flying airplanes and running an ultramarathon. Priests have many of the same responsibilities, but they each bring their own flavor and personality to their ministry.

Third, *you become who you hang around*. Hanging around other men discerning the priesthood, seminarians, and priests helps you to form a shared identity. You can ask yourself deeper questions about yourself such as "Can I see myself with this group of people?" "Would I fit in?" "How similar or different am I from them?" Considering the priesthood can be difficult, but it doesn't have to be done in isolation.

In this way, being part of a community of like-minded men can provide much-needed support, fellowship, and friendship. People receive support from multiple sources—family, friends, coworkers, etc. It is human nature to seek support from people with similar experiences. Parents enjoy talking about the trials of parenthood with other parents because there are some things that only another parent can understand. Military men and women seek out other military personnel because of the shared understanding of their unique experiences. Similarly, hearing and following a call from God is an experience that not everyone in your life can relate to and provide you with appropriate support. You can only find the shared understanding and support in other men who have gone through the discernment process before or are going through it right now.

Fourth and finally, engaging in all these activities—praying about God's will in your life, joining a men's discernment group, attending a vocations discernment retreat, talking with the vocation director, visiting a seminary, and talking with current priests and seminarians—creates what psychologists call *behavioral momentum*. When we have a goal, we usually think about our goal and assess our abilities and the barriers to accomplishing the goal. Let's take running a marathon as an example. Choosing to run a marathon is a goal that originates in some prior set of thoughts. You may want to lose some weight, become more physically fit, and/or desire a new challenge for yourself. Either way, the point is that you think about running a marathon before actually running the marathon.

You then start to assess your abilities—I have run a 5k before; I am pretty good with training. And then doubt creeps in—"Can I do this? What if I get hurt while training? I don't know if I can maintain the training regimen." All these questions occur in your head, before you log even one mile on the track. To accomplish the goal, you have to get outside of your head and engage in actions that will help you achieve the goal. The actions start to build momentum. For running a marathon, you might start by buying new running shoes, setting a training schedule, and then running two times a week. Those actions lay the foundation for subsequent actions, which may be more complex and rigorous, such as running four times a week.

The same principle applies to discerning the priesthood. We have already established that thinking about the priesthood causes reluctance and some men completely rule out the possibility without ever trying. In other words, men spend too much time in their head, which unnecessarily complicates discernment and contributes to self-imposed psychological barriers to the priesthood. Create some behavioral momentum by getting outside of your head and engaging in the tried and true behaviors that provide support, direction, and clarity.

A KEY QUESTION TO ASK YOURSELF IS – "WHAT IS STOPPING ME FROM TAKING THAT NEXT ACTIVE STEP IN YOUR PRAYERFUL CONSIDERATION OF THE PRIESTHOOD?"

Think about it. Is God stopping you? No. The National Guard? Nope. Your pastor? Probably not. The weather? Traffic? No and no. As you create behavioral momentum by engaging in activities that promote your vocational decision-making, you naturally stop doing activities that cloud your discernment. You will begin to notice that you aren't as motivated to do things like party all night, endlessly play video games, anxiously check text messages, count social media "likes", hang out with non-supportive friends, obsessively assess your financial investments, and the list goes on. You know God is working in your life when priorities and motivations shift.

So many activities confuse discernment. Yet, nothing is stopping you from doing activities that clarify your discernment. For every man thinking of the priesthood as a possible vocation, a key to turning your discernment into an enjoyable journey with fruitful learning experiences is to engage in behaviors that are aligned with the priesthood, with other like-minded men. In other words, you have to jump into the pool!

SIMPLE AND ACTIVE
1. Think of discernment as an active process rather than a passive one.

2. Identify how you can be more active by engaging in vocation-supporting activities. Below is a list, to which we refer throughout the rest of the book. You have lots of options and we encourage you to start with small, concrete, and reasonable goals to engage in these spiritual practices. Doing too much, too soon is typically unsustainable, especially without support and direction.

LIST OF VOCATION-SUPPORTING ACTIVITIES

✝ Attend a men's discernment retreat.

✝ Meet with your diocesan vocations director or a trusted priest.

✝ Engage in spiritual direction. A spiritual director is usually a priest that helps you to identify and to understand God's voice in your life. It is confusing to discern your vocation on your own; a spiritual director provides clarity and support.

✝ Visit your diocesan seminary for a tour and to meet the seminary faculty and seminarians.

✝ Deepen your prayer life.

- Increase your mass attendance during the week.
- Pray the rosary at least once a week. Mary loves to help us.
- Spend fifteen minutes in adoration at least once a week. Adoration allows you simply to gaze at God in awe and receive graces from being in God's presence.
- Take ten minutes to sit quietly and engage in mental prayer. Mental prayer is simply having a conversation with God. You can have a conversation with God at any time and any place, but it requires silence.

3, Get your calendar out and plan to do one of those activities today and over the next three days. Good habits are often established after twenty-one days.

- Your immediate goal is to do an activity today.
- Your short-term goal is do an activity every day for three days.
- Your intermediate goal is do an activity every day for a week.
- Your ultimate goal is to take on the 21-day challenge. Do an activity every day for twenty-one days straight.

Here is a simple table to help you with your goals. Writing the activity down, putting it into your schedule, and tracking your reactions is a tried and true way to stay committed and accountable to goals. We recommend that you use this table to enhance your commitment and accountability. We provided an example and some blank spaces for you to fill-in.

DISCERNMENT-ENCOURAGING ACTIVITY	DATE/TIME	REACTIONS
EXAMPLE: Spend 15 minutes in adoration	Thursday at 3:00pm	Took a break in-between classes to go to adoration. I didn't want to go at first, but I had it in my schedule. It was quiet and I had some time to clear my head and ask God for help. It was a good start.

CHAPTER 3

PERPETUAL DISCERNER OR
RELUCTANT HERO?

Put the idea of priesthood aside for a moment. Just focus on everything that goes into making a career choice. Making a career choice involves understanding yourInterests: sports, mechanics, helping others, entrepreneurial, politics, etc.

- ✟ Values: service, status, flexibility, independence, teams, etc.
- ✟ Abilities: What are you good at? What career can you perform well?
- ✟ Barriers: money, opportunities, success
- ✟ Supports: friends, family, community, resources

As we mentioned in the Introduction, we are asking you to think beyond your career choice and to consider your deeper *vocation* from a Catholic perspective. Identifying your vocation entails understanding all of the things that go into a career choice—interests, values, abilities, barriers, and supports. In addition, a Catholic perspective of vocation includes identifying what you want to do with your life, and relating that to what you think God wants you to do. We hit a sweet spot when our desires and goals align with God's desires and plan for us. Making a career choice and considering your vocation takes time and effort. You do not want to rush into a big decision.

We didn't just snap our fingers and become psychologists overnight. Of course, we engaged in formal study and training that took time and a lot of work. For a long time, we simply referred to ourselves as professional students because of the amount of time we spent in school. Prior to study, we also discussed our goals and interests with people. We prayed about our futures and asked God what He wanted from us. We studied philosophy, considered other options, and reviewed the data about psychologists such as salary ranges, job prospects, types of employment, and the various subfields. There was a logic to the process as we did our due diligence and gathered information to help in our decision-making. For us, choosing psychology was not only a career choice but also an identification of a vocation, as we felt that God wanted us to help others by putting our faith into action through our profession.

Depending on the year and source, statistics indicate that 50–80% of college students change their major at least once. On average, college students will change their major three to five times before they graduate. Some people scratch their heads out of frustration and confusion with college students because of apparent indecision. But there is nothing wrong with trial and error learning. The point of those two statistical examples is to show you that choosing a vocation is not always logical, rational, clear, organized, or linear. It does take time and you may get confused or feel uncertain along the way. Where you end up is not always predictable.

Psychologist Dr. John Krumboltz calls choosing a vocation an unpredictable *journey*. He makes some important points. First, you are likely to hold several careers, jobs, and vocations throughout your life and sometimes all at the same time. He has a great way of describing his career journey (2009, p. 136):

I personally have been employed as a gardener, magazine sales person, chauffeur, farmer, drill press operator, aluminum foundry worker, cereal packager, railroad loader, elevator operator, chemist's assistant, pancake taster, book publisher's assistant, radio announcer, teaching assistant, tennis coach, camp counselor, career counselor, high school counselor, algebra teacher, military officer, test construction specialist, research psychologist, professor, and author. I did not, and never could have, predicted this pattern of employment. And who knows what I will do next?

Dr. Krumboltz emphasizes that we can enjoy the journey, learn a lot along the way, and appreciate the fact that we do not need to have everything figured out. None of those jobs were a waste of time because he learned something important about himself, the world of work, or life in general with each job, which helped him make subsequent decisions.

Let's tie up a couple of threads. It would be nice to 1) explore our vocation and come to a general conclusion about a major, career, profession in a short period of time, and 2) enjoy and appreciation the exploration while understanding that there is still a long, unknown journey ahead of us. Sounds pretty good. However, and this is an emphatic HOWEVER, men that we have talked to about the priesthood rarely go through such an enjoyable, time-limited decision-making process.

ARE YOU A RELUCTANT HERO OR PERPETUAL DISCERNER?

There is a character archetype in books and movies called the *Reluctant Hero*. A Reluctant Hero is an ordinary man, i.e., "the every man," who is not perfect and has some clear faults. What usually happens is that there is a conflict or problem of some kind and this man gets pulled into the conflict. He is reluctant, tries to resist, and comes up with all sorts of reasons why he is not best suited to solve the problem. Inevitably, the reluctant man gets pulled into the action and exhibits heroism. Frodo from the *Lord of the Rings* is an excellent example of the Reluctant Hero. Men who consider the priesthood are certainly reluctant to pursue the priesthood. You are likely experiencing reluctance. And to be fair, some reluctance is normal and expected. As described above, part of making a decision is exploring and learning over a period of time.

Yet, we have noticed that many men exhibit an immense and even insurmountable reluctance to the idea of the priesthood. Some of the reluctance stems from the reasons we outlined in the Introduction (e.g., little money, too many rules). The reluctance mutates into a chronic state of agonizing exploration and indecision. It is not uncommon for us to talk with men who have been "on the fence" about the priesthood for ten, fifteen, even twenty years. These men have gone back and forth countless times with **Questions**—should I be a priest? **Conclusions**—I will revisit the idea of the priesthood in a couple of years, **Speculations**—maybe, just maybe, God is calling me to be a priest, and **Half-Baked Decisions**—I will just keep praying and hope something happens. All this activity is exhausting and does not lead to anything except frustration and continued uncertainty. We have heard vocation directors (priests in charge of talking to men about the priesthood) categorize these kinds of men as "*Perpetual Discerners.*"

Perpetual discerners turn a decision about the priesthood into a constant state of reluctance, agony, and endless debate with God, themselves, and possibly even friends and family. The result of perpetual discernment is that men are stuck feeling ambivalence, and ambivalence is a feeling that directly contributes to inaction. On the one hand, they feel a deep and constant urge to explore the priesthood, enter a seminary, or become a priest. On the other hand, they resist the urge, identify all of the reasons not to enter a seminary, and continually decide to take more time. Recall from Chapter 2 how important we considered action to be in discernment. Therefore, we obviously caution against putting yourself in a cycle of ambivalent inaction. We have seen men literally double over in physical pain because of their perpetual discernment. The decision to take more time becomes the biggest decision that men make. In the process, men turn a potentially enjoyable, educational journey of decision-making that can align their goals with those of God into a drawn-out, painful experience.

We like to use sports metaphors. Think of running a marathon. A marathon covers 26.2 miles from the starting line to the finish line. You run from point A to point B. You go toward a destination, accomplish a difficult task, and feel good (but definitely tired) about that accomplishment. Now, imagine running 26.2 miles on a treadmill. You run and run and run, but do not actually go anywhere. You stay in the same place despite the buckets of sweat, which suggest otherwise. To make the connection clear, running a marathon on a treadmill is like perpetual discernment. You exert a lot of effort and energy. You feel tired afterwards. But, you do not actually go anywhere. We want you to go somewhere and experience a sense of accomplishment for your efforts.

Remember *Lord of the Rings* again. Frodo eventually leaves the Shire and embarks on a grand adventure to get rid of the Ring. Reluctant Heroes get involved in the action, help solve the problem, and resolve the conflict. In our clinical experiences conducting psychological evaluations with men applying to the seminary, we noticed that many applicants are in their mid-20s and 30s. We ask every applicant why they are applying to the seminary *now*. What makes the time right—

now? And all of them start to answer that question by saying something along the lines of "I first felt called to be a priest as a child, in high school, ten years ago, fifteen years ago, etc. I delayed. I ran from the call. I tried to ignore it, but it kept coming back." All of these men seemed a little tired, which makes sense if you have been running from God for years! But, they have moved forward and made progress by taking the next step and applying to the seminary. These men are good examples of Reluctant Heroes.

Reluctant Heroes do not feel ambivalent and are not passive. We have seen the look of peace, relief, and excitement on men's faces. They smile brightly and widely, if not a bit wearily. Reluctant Heroes have generated positive behavioral momentum by engaging in the vocation-supporting activities on the list. The men who broke through the negative cycle of perpetual discernment were not lazy, unproductive couch potatoes. Many applicants to the seminary are accomplished professionals in their respective fields. They have obtained bachelor's and graduate degrees in theology, philosophy, engineering, biology, education. They are smart and educated. Most, if not all applicants have a strong service record—volunteering in their parishes, mission trips, and campus ministry. Some have served our country in the military. They are caring and want to help others. All applicants describe a faithful prayer life and connection to God. They go to mass, Eucharistic adoration, confession, lead Bible studies, pray the rosary and Divine Mercy Chaplet. They are prayerful and spiritual. In other words, the Church is filled with smart, educated, service-oriented, and prayerful men that hear God's voice to discern the priesthood.

We firmly believe that there are good men out there who can make great priests. You may be one of these men that God is calling. Examine your inner experiences and be honest with yourself. If you look inward and notice that, more often than not, you are ambivalent, angst-filled, pained, restless, and stuck in a particular life stage—those feelings are indicators that you aren't following God's will and fall in the perpetual discernment category. Conversely, if you have a sense of peace, contentment, relief, and anticipation about the next steps in your journey although you have some uncertainty—those feelings are indicators that you're following God's will and fall in the reluctant hero category.

AN IMPORTANT QUESTION TO ASK YOURSELF RIGHT NOW IS- - ARE YOU A PERPETUAL DISCERNER OR A RELUCTANT HERO?

BREAKING THE BARRIER

Yes, *The Lord of the Rings* is an epic. Running a marathon is an epic run. But, giving the priesthood serious consideration doesn't have to be a drawn-out, grueling process of epic proportions. In fact, we argue that enough men are perpetual discerners that a myth has developed. The myth is that you have to go through an agonizing and confusing process of discernment to be a priest, as if it is some kind of a prerequisite. That myth becomes a psychological barrier to progressing in your discernment. Considering the priesthood does not have to be that way. We want to bust that myth and break down the barrier. Many men are reluctant to take the next steps but do eventually take action. They overcome their reluctance and embrace the uncertainty of the future. The men that went on a discernment retreat, visited the seminary, applied to the seminary all felt better about their decision-making because of engaging in those actions. A key to breaking the barriers is to turn perpetual discernment into reluctant heroism. If some men can break the barriers, we believe that more men with a call can follow suit.

SIMPLE AND ACTIVE

Our simple approach to discernment entails getting past the common barriers that plague men.

1. Do not think that your discernment has to be long, agonizing, and heart-wrenching.
2. Do not foreclose on the priesthood without even trying activities that are aligned with the priesthood.
3. Do not stay inside your head and let your own thoughts block you from pursuing what God may be calling you to.
4. The next part of our approach is to engage in the tried and true activities that priests, bishops, and other seminarians have consistently recommended as helpful to discerning a vocation.
5. If you are a perpetual discerner, your next step might be to take the plunge and apply to the seminary. What else is there for you to do?
6. If you are a reluctant hero, your next steps might be to talk with a priest, visit seminary, and/or go on a discernment retreat. Go deeper and work through the reluctance.
7. You can also revisit the list of **Vocations-Supporting Activities** from Chapter 2. Identify and engage in the activity from the list that will help you move from point A to point B.

CHAPTER 4

How Do I *Know* That Becoming a Priest Is My Vocation?

H ave you ever had an experience in your life when you just *knew*? Acute experiences of knowledge provide clarity and direction in our lives. For example, maybe you knew that you had to study harder to pass a test. The realization that you needed to study harder for a test was accompanied by a realization that you needed to spend longer hours in the library. You then have to inform your friends that you cannot hang out on a Saturday afternoon. Knowledge is a gift but can also make a decision more difficult.

At some point in your life, perhaps you just knew that it was time to break up with a girlfriend. Knowing that you have to break up with a girlfriend comes with feelings of grief and heartache that can delay the decision. Knowledge is important, but we often have to make decisions without full, acute knowledge of the pros and cons, consequences, and impact of the decisions. Life is full of situations and questions that require sustained effort to search for knowledge. In other words, we have to act without full knowledge and while still searching for information.

For example, there are bigger questions that we confront throughout our lives, which challenge us to search for knowledge about ourselves and purpose in life. Who am I? What am I supposed to do with my life? What is my purpose? Why am I here? What brings me joy and happiness? Those are *existen-*

tial questions. Existential questions are deep, thought-pro-voking, and essential questions to grapple with and to answer in your life. Arriving at answers to those questions takes time, study, introspection, prayer, discussion with friends, class-mates, teachers, and mentors. We are hardwired to answer existential questions. Honestly, time spent searching for an-swers to those questions is part of what makes life interesting and fun as well as confusing and angst-filled.

GOD WANTS US TO KNOW WHO WE ARE, WHAT OUR PURPOSE IS, AND HOW TO OBTAIN HAPPI-NESS IN OUR LIVES.

HOW DO I KNOW?! I WANT TO KNOW!

Yes, it is fun and angst-filled to get wrapped up in the big existential questions of life. Questions about our vocation are similar. Recall from earlier in the book that figuring out your vocation is a combination of answering two key questions: 1) What do I want to do? and 2) What does God want me to do? The congruence between the answers to those two questions provides critical insight into your vocation. However, a calling from God can be surprising and confusing. We want to be cer-tain that what we think God is calling us to do, God is in fact calling us to do.

One of our favorite paintings is the *Calling of St. Matthew* by Caravaggio. We encourage you to take a good look at it and reflect on it yourself. In our study of the painting, we noticed a clear sense of humor. Jesus comes into the room and points at St. Matthew. The message to St. Matthew is clear: "Follow me" (Mt. 9:9). St. Matthew's response provides the comic relief. Keep in mind, at the time Jesus calls him, St. Matthew was no saint at all. He was a no-good tax collector, and tax collectors were despised in that time and culture. St. Matthew rightfully points at himself and exhibits a quizzical facial expression that communicates "Who? Me?" At that moment, St. Matthew must have been thinking: there's no way that Jesus is calling *me* to follow *Him*. St. Matthew was undoubtedly surprised that Jesus was calling him. Simply put, if you have thought that God is calling you to the priesthood, you have probably felt like St. Matthew. You have asked yourself the same question that St. Matthew asked himself: "Who? Me?" As a result, you want some evidence.

ONE OF THE BIGGEST QUESTIONS MEN HAVE WHEN DISCERNING THE PRIESTHOOD IS, "HOW DO I *KNOW* THAT GOD IS CALLING ME TO THE PRIESTHOOD?"

Asking God to confirm your vocation is pretty reasonable. If a college sends an acceptance letter to confirm your admittance, maybe God should send a confirmation email or text about your vocation. If you are going to commit yourself to something for the rest of your life, you want to know that it is the right decision. These points are well-taken. A certain level of confidence that God is calling you to the priesthood is important. After all, the whole goal of discernment is to deepen your understanding of God's will in your life and live out that calling. God doesn't play a cat and mouse game either. He wants you to know your vocation so that you can live it out as fully and passionately as possible.

A THOUGHT EXPERIMENT

Take a moment to think about the range of possible vocations. Doctor, lawyer, engineer, financial analyst, accountant, professor, father, business owner, dentist, youth minister, counselor, religious education teacher, lector, etc. There are many possible vocations but let's take one for the purposes of this thought experiment—dentist. Imagine you are praying to God about becoming a dentist and you felt that God wanted you to become a dentist. Your prayer sounds like this: "God, I want to be a dentist, and I feel like you want me to be a dentist. However, before I become a dentist, I need 100% proof from you that I am really supposed to become a dentist. I won't go to dentistry school until I have that proof. Please include in your evidence to me information about what kind of dentistry practice I will have in five to ten years, how many patients per week I will see, and how many years I will practice." That prayer sounds unreasonable and irrational. The prayer basically asks God to a) confirm the vocational choice, b) tell you very specific information about the future, and c) it gives God an ultimatum—tell me this information or I won't follow through. (For the record, we don't think giving God ultimatums is a good idea.)

Many of the men that want to *know* whether they are called to the priesthood aren't looking for a boost in confidence or a bit of inspiration. They get bogged down by seeking "proof" that God is calling them to the priesthood. Not just any proof, but rock-solid, air-tight, explicit proof. This need for 100% proof seems specific to a priestly vocation. Men don't seek such proof for other decisions in their life. Take the dentist example from above. We would venture to conclude that nobody, or very few people, made such a prayer to God about dentistry or any other career. It just doesn't make sense to talk to God that way. There is some amount of uncertainty when we make big decisions in our life. Uncertainty is inevitable.

We started this chapter by talking about experiences of acute knowledge. Yes, it would be great if an angel from our Lord appeared with glad tidings to tell you what you are supposed to do with your life and to confirm if you are supposed to be a priest. Imagine how easy it would be to know God's will if a dove descended from the sky and whispered in your ear, "My good and faithful servant, you shall become a priest." If you had those remarkable experiences, you would obtain the unquestionable knowledge of God's will.

THE BOTTOM LINE IS THAT MEN GET STUCK IN THEIR DISCERNMENT BECAUSE OF THEIR IRRATIONAL NEED FOR 100% PROOF OF A PRIESTLY VOCATION.

The subsequent sections of this chapter break down this irrational and unhelpful barrier. We provide simple and active ways to move forward.

STARTING SMALL. STARTING WITH SERVICE.

Big questions can be intimidating, scary, confusing, and difficult to answer. Knowing whether or not God wants you to be a priest is no exception. In 2009, two psychologists set out to describe what a calling means from a psychological perspective. Their names are Drs. Ryan Duffy and Bryan Dik from the University of Florida and Colorado State University, respectively. Their ambitions were high because most psychologists doubt matters of faith, spirituality, and religion. They identified two key indicators of an authentic calling. First, they said that an authentic calling entails a "transcendent summons."

For most men, the calling to the priesthood does not include an angel messenger or a parting of clouds with God's thunderous voice. Priests often talk about hearing the voice of God calling them to the priesthood. But, they describe God's voice as a small, faint, but very persistent whisper. Some men even considered the voice to be incredibly annoying—similar to your mother nagging you to take out the garbage. Stop it! Leave me alone! Go away! I'll get to it later! A transcendent summons is that voice from God urging you to do something of meaning and purpose in your life. Many of you are reading this book because of that transcendent summons.

Second, Drs. Duffy and Dik stated that the transcendent summons pushes the individual to help others. The second indicator of an authentic calling is that you feel drawn to serving and helping other people. This makes a lot of sense when you think about the role of the priest. A priest serves God by serving God's people. A priest is meant to minister to the needs of other people and to do good in the world. Most discernment retreats and talks emphasize the need to hear God's voice. We agree, and we bet that most of you have heard God's voice. Asking God to speak louder, clearer, and with more information is one way to seek clarification on your possible vocation to the priesthood. Another way to answer the question about whether God is calling you to the priesthood is to engage in acts of service. Taken together, hearing voices from God to live a life of meaning and service is not crazy, it is extraordinary.

You do not have to be a fortune teller who knows his future with 100% certainty. The calling to the priesthood is sometimes best revealed through simple acts of service. One of the great modern examples of discernment through service is Blessed Pier Giorgio Frassati. Frassati was a strong, young, and athletic man. He lived in Italy in the early 1920s. He was a mountaineer, who regularly scaled mountains with nothing more than a pick-ax and some rope. Apart from being an all-around stud, Frassati came from a wealthy Italian family that had deep political ties, power, and influence. But Frassati did not get wrapped up in prestige, wealth, and politicking. He was committed to a life of service out of his devotion to God.

Frassati would sneak off to serve the poor, out of the eyes of the public and without his family knowing his whereabouts. He offered food, money, kindness, and compassion to those in need. Frassati pursued God's will by getting involved and *putting his beliefs into practice.*

Frassati's life is an excellent example of simple and active discernment. His family wanted him to be an engineer, politician, journalist, or businessman, something worthy of the social status of the Frassati family. Yet, Blessed Pier knew with quiet confidence what he was supposed to do with his life—serve others. Although his parents and friends constantly questioned his intellect, decision-making, and vocation, Blessed Pier carried on with his activities with full quiet confidence based on certain knowledge of his service-oriented call. He teaches us that every act of service to another person becomes a moment for deeper understanding. Something as easy as praying for a family member or sending an encouraging text message to a friend can help you discover God's will in your life. We believe that these small deeds will point you in the right direction. They will build on each other, motivate you, and push you forward in your discernment. We also believe that helping others is a better way to spend time in discernment than continually asking God for more proof.

Back to the million-dollar question at hand, "How do I *know* that God is calling me to the priesthood?" A good place to start to answer that question is through simple acts of service. From there you can begin to take more concrete steps, such as becoming more involved in service activities. Mission trips, shifts at the soup kitchen, volunteering at a nursing home, tutoring a student, and visiting a troubled friend are some examples of service. Sometimes the big questions of life are answered best when you get outside of your head and start living a life of service.

HELP WITH YOUR DECISION

You might be familiar with the movie *Cast Away*, a famous film starring Tom Hanks as the character Chuck Noland, an engineer whose plane crashes in the Pacific Ocean, leaving him to fend for himself on an uninhabited island. Chuck spends four years of his life on the island without any human interaction, alone, isolated, and fighting for his survival. His only companion is a volleyball named Wilson. Chuck's relationship with Wilson grows throughout the film. He starts talking to Wilson, getting into arguments, and developing a strong emotional bond with the volleyball. *Cast Away* highlights the importance of our social relationships in providing meaning, purpose, and direction in life. Chuck is so desperate for social interaction that he befriends a volleyball.

Sometimes when men discern the priesthood, they can start to feel a little bit like Chuck when he washed up on the uninhabited island. They are exploring new, uncharted territory, and there is no one to help. They might not know anyone else who is thinking about the priesthood and feel alone or isolated. As a result, men discerning the priesthood might not know who to contact, call, or bounce ideas off. They get wrapped up in their thoughts, with no outside perspective. Men start to think that their vocation is something to be figured out on their own—on an uninhabited island in the middle of the Pacific Ocean.

If there is anything to take from a quick viewing of *Cast Away*, it is the power and importance of our relationships with others. Fortunately, discernment of the priesthood is not meant to be done alone and important decisions are not meant to be made in total isolation. This would be scary, confusing, and might hold you back. The Church is designed to help and support you. We are encouraging you to call on the support of the Church to help you simplify the discernment process. There are people who can be there to support you in your discernment—priests, vocations directors, current seminarians, discernment groups, church members, and religious communities. You are definitely not alone. One of the best ways to begin understanding whether you are called to the priesthood is by connecting with people in the Church. The Church has a responsibility to help you through this process.

A fresh set of eyes and the opportunity to give your vocation a little air time can go a long way. Every priest and seminarian has been through the process of discernment and is still discerning. At one point, every one of them was in your shoes, trying to figure out what to do with their lives. Surrounding yourself with individuals who have dealt with the same questions, hearing their stories, and reflecting on your own experiences will provide you with clarity. The idea here is simple, and it works for pretty much all vocations. If you want to be a dentist, talk to a dentist. If you want to be a fireman, talk to a fireman. When we were thinking of becoming psychologists, we spoke to other psychologists. If you want to be a priest, you should connect with priests.

PERHAPS A BETTER QUESTION THAN "HOW DO *I* KNOW I'M CALLED TO THE PRIESTHOOD?" IS "HOW DO *WE* KNOW I'M CALLED TO THE PRIESTHOOD?"

LOOK IN THE OPPOSITE DIRECTION

To quickly recap, we have talked about three ways to help you tackle big questions about your vocation (1) listening to God's voice, (2) serving others and, (3) connecting with people in the Church who have gone through what you are going through, such as seminarians and priests. There is a fourth way that is often overlooked. I would imagine that you have had the experience of crossing a road before. Usually, when little kids learn how to cross the road, they are taught to look left, right, then left again. Fast forward to the teenage years, and we usually hear this message again when learning to drive. Before pulling out into traffic, aspiring drivers are taught to look left, look right, then check left again. The idea here is that you check left first because the cars coming from the left are in the lane closest to you. Then you cast your gaze to the right, making sure that there are no cars in the far lane. And finally, you recheck the left, for good measure, to make sure the coast is clear. If you're going to pull out into traffic, you need to make sure you check both ways.

A lot of times when it comes to the priesthood, men only look one way. They cast their vision to the left, only looking for the 100% proof, confirmatory evidence that God is calling them to the priesthood. However, there is another direction for men to look.

INSTEAD OF ASKING, "WHAT PROOF DO I HAVE THAT GOD IS CALLING ME TO THE PRIESTHOOD?", ASK YOURSELF, "WHAT PROOF IS THERE THAT I'M NOT BEING CALLED TO THE PRIESTHOOD?"

This technique flips proof on its head and gives a fuller picture. It looks to the right, not just to the left. We call this approach looking for disconfirmatory evidence. Rather than always focusing on the "proof," it is equally helpful to ask, "Why not? Is there anything that is preventing me from becoming a priest?" If God has not given you a resounding "NO!" then the priesthood might still be in the cards. Looking both ways before crossing the street is a must. Do not forget to look both ways when discerning the priesthood. Searching for both confirmatory and disconfirmatory evidence is helpful as you wonder if the priesthood is for you. Avoid exclusively looking for confirmatory evidence as disconfirmatory evidence also provides valuable information about your vocation. The Church can help with both.

SIMPLE AND ACTIVE

Continuing to identify and overcome common barriers is the next step in taking a more simple and active approach to your discernment.

1. Do not fall into the trap of trying to know your vocation with 100% certainty.
2. Do not isolate yourself from other people in the Church, leaving yourself alone to figure out your vocation.
3. Do not only seek out confirmatory evidence that God is calling you to be a priest.

The next step is to take a more realistic, action-based, and socially-connected approach to discerning the priesthood.

1. Look for two key indicators of an authentic calling that will clarify your vocation—God's quiet, persistent voice and acts of service to others.
2. Connect with people in the Church who can help support you in your discernment. We recommend that you find the vocation director in your diocese, contact him, and set up a meeting. Here is a link to a website, which helps you to find the closest vocation director to you: http://www.diocesan-priest.com/map-united-states/
3. When crossing the street, make sure you look both ways. Look for both confirmatory evidence AND disconfirmatory evidence that God is calling you the priesthood. If you haven't received a resounding "NO!" the priesthood might still be in the cards.

CHAPTER 5

MASCULINITY AND THE PRIESTHOOD

L ast year, we went to a few Catholic high schools to talk to young men about their vocations. We wanted to gauge their interest in the priesthood and hear some of the obstacles they have encountered. The young men were candid with us and identified several barriers to pursuing a possible vocation to the priesthood. Many of the barriers were so important and prevalent among the young men that they could not be easily brushed aside. The barriers ran deep. To briefly recap: lack of money, status, and sex, as well as the perceptions of the priesthood as boring, repetitive, and without risk and adventure.

We realized that many of these barriers were related to a much bigger topic. The young men were not able to articulate how all of those barriers added up to a bigger barrier— namely, their ideas of manhood. Taking a job or initiating a career that does not include money and status as well as a life without adventure and sex are all counter to prominent ideas of manhood. Therefore, those barriers are particularly powerful because they tap into what it means to be a man in today's society.

We discussed deep, existential questions in previous chapters. This book started by asking you to think about your vocation—what do you want with life and what is God calling you to do? This chapter continues along those lines by asking you some more thought-provoking questions.

WHAT KIND OF MAN ARE YOU? WHAT KIND OF MAN DO YOU WANT TO BE?

Questions do not get much deeper. Grappling with these questions and coming to some answers make life more intentional and self-directed. We have asked men those two questions in therapy, focus groups, on retreats, in friendships. Men react to the questions in various ways—with excitement, confusion, silence, cringing, deep exploration, but never with boredom.

Follow us through this chapter as we go down this rabbit hole of manhood, vocation, and priesthood—weighty topics, for sure, that are easy to ignore and not discuss. We believe that understanding who you are as a man is essential to understanding what to do with your life and the calling to the priesthood.

THE *MAN'S* MAN

There is not a one size fits all model of manhood. However, our culture puts forth common traits and popular stereotypes that communicate to men messages about what it means to be a man. Let's take a look at a few of these messages. Depending on your age and sense of cultural history, you may recall The Marlboro Man and John Wayne from the 1950s, 60s, and 70s. Those two guys were tough and stoic, men of few words but forceful action. Most men growing up during those decades wanted to be just like John Wayne. He was an actor and cultural hero. He set the standard for what it meant to be a man's man.

In the 1980s and 1990s, our culture focused on "bigger is better." Men like Sylvester Stallone and Arnold Schwarzenegger were box-office giants. They were tough, muscular, and destroyed everything in their paths. We recently watched a docuseries about toys from the 1980s. The toy developers were interviewed and described focus groups with young boys that they conducted to generate toy ideas. According to the toy developers, the young boys kept using the word 'power' while playing with toys in the focus groups. Power over their parents, teachers, older siblings, etc. The company soon produced a toy for boys called *He-Man,* with the catchphrase "I have the power!" There is little subtlety in the toy's name and plenty of redundancy as both "he" and "man" were used to emphasize the manliness of the toy. And of course, to be a he-man, you needed the power. Not much has changed in the modern day. Athletes are adored for their physical abilities, physique, and commercial appeal. CEOs and politicians are envied for their power and influence.

Those popular cultural images of manhood match up with the psychological study of men over the last thirty years. In the early 2000s, psychologist Dr. James Mahalik at Boston College conducted a study to identify the most popular "masculinity norms" in the United States. He defined masculinity norms as the expectations that people have for men in society. Dr. Mahalik's study found fifteen masculinity norms, including: Winning, Emotional Control, Risk-Taking, Violence, Power over Women, Dominance, Playboy, Self-Reliance, Primacy of Work, Disdain for Homosexuals, and Pursuit of Status. Even after fifteen years of researchers trying to disprove his findings, these same eleven themes have withstood the test of time.

Around the same time as Dr. Mahalik, another psychologist named Dr. Ronald Levant from the University of Akron was working on a similar question: what are the traditional roles and norms for men in the United States? Dr. Levant found seven traditional roles: Avoidance of Femininity, Fear and Hatred of Homosexuals, Extreme Self-Reliance, Aggression, Dominance, Non-Relational Attitudes Towards Sexuality, and Restrictive Emotionality. These seven roles have held up over the course of fifteen years, across several studies with thousands of men.

Let's put the two lists together. The men in all of these studies believe that society expects them to win, maintain emotional control, take risks, be aggressive or violent, exert power over women, display dominance in relationships and work, be sexually active but non-committal, self-reliant, make work a top priority, disdain homosexuals, pursue status, and avoid anything considered feminine. Those are the expectations of men in our society.

We believe that list is incomplete at best, and some norms are downright scary at worst. Some very important expectations are missing from the list. Why are men not expected to be spiritual or religious? Caring or loving? Compassionate and empathetic? Servant-leaders?

THE CATHOLIC MAN CRISIS

Let's be clear that we are not "throwing the baby out with the bathwater." We recognize that there are some positive aspects of societal expectations of manhood. Indeed, learning to compete, being willing to protect and serve others, providing for one's family, and autonomously solving problems are admirable traits. A lot of men become soldiers, police officers, firemen, loving husbands and fathers by positively putting those expectations into everyday practice. We encourage you to think deeply about how you may be exhibiting such expectations in both positive and negative ways. Of course, keep the positive, get rid of the negative.

The Catholic Church, however, has recognized that there

is something wrong with the secular society's expectations of manhood. Pope Francis, in his 2014 book *Joy of the Gospel* (p. 61), listed machismo along with alcoholism and domestic violence among several social and cultural "deficiencies" in need of healing. That's how serious the Pope considers this problem to be. A year later in 2015, Bishop Thomas Olmsted of the Diocese of Phoenix picked up where the Pope left off. Bishop Olmsted wrote a powerful and impassioned letter to Catholic men entitled *Into the Breach*. Bishop Olmsted called men into action. We draw your attention to one quote from Bishop Olmsted from his letter to men:

Looking to what the secular world holds up as "manly" is to look at shadows—or even at outright counterfeits—of masculinity. No athlete, no matter how many awards; no political leader, no matter the power he wields; no performer, business man, or celebrity, no matter how much adored; no physical attribute or muscle mass; no intelligence or talent; no prizes or achievements can bestow masculinity on a man. The idolatry of celebrities at this time is a particular temptation, but to build one's masculine identity on such fleeting models is to build an identity on sand. My Catholic sons and brothers, we can only build a certain foundation for masculinity on the rock, Jesus Christ. We look to our Savior to be transformed in Him, to be the men we are called to be, and to let others see Him in us.

It is clear that society does not expect men to be religious, spiritual, service-oriented, and self-sacrificial. Those expectations have not made the secular society's "manhood" lists. It is human nature that people behave in ways that are expected of them. For example, if a teacher sets high expectations for academic performance, students will generally change their behaviors to meet those academic milestones. Conversely, if a teacher has low expectations, students will do the minimum amount of work, knowing that the bar is low.

There seems to be a similar dynamic at play with men and religion. Men are not expected to be religious, spiritual, service-oriented, and self-sacrificial, so many men are not doing religious, spiritual, service-oriented, and self-sacrificial activities. First, look broadly at some statistics. According to statistics from the PEW Center on Religion and Public Life (2015), it is well-known that more women are affiliated with a major world religion compared to men in the United States and similar western countries (e.g., United Kingdom). Similarly, more men identified as atheists and religiously unaffiliated compared to women in the United States in 2015. Fewer men, compared to women, attend weekly religious services, pray, meditate, and read scripture on a daily or weekly basis.

Those broad statistics have trickled down to Catholic men. You may have heard of the New Evangelization in the Catholic Church. Many big-name Catholic speakers and authors have spoken at length about the need for the Catholic Church to re-Christianize those people who have left the Catholic Church. What has not been spoken about at length is that the New Evangelization requires a new "*emangelization*."

There is a website, www.newemangelization.com, devoted to addressing the need to bring men back to the Catholic Church. Consider the following statistics from the website:

✝ Only about $^1/_3$ of Catholic men (36%) say they attend mass on a weekly basis.

✝ Almost half of Catholic men do not engage in a routine of prayer; praying only "occasionally or sometimes" or "seldom or never."

✝ Approximately 40% of casually Catholic men believe that Catholicism does not have a "greater share of truths than other religions."

✞   Catholic men are less passionate about faith than other Christian men. Only 48% of Catholic men feel that "religion is very important in their lives" compared to 74% of Evangelical men.

✞   Only about 4 in 10 Catholic men (43%) have a certain belief in a personal God; this compares to 73% of evangelical men.

✞   Less than half of Catholic men (48%) pray outside of worship services, which compares to 71% of Evangelical men.[1] What is a simple explanation for such statistics? Men don't have time for religious and spiritual matters because they are too busy trying to meet the societal expectations of manhood. Who has time for church when you are working eighty hours a week, chasing multiple women, trying to figure everything out on your own, and pursuing everything and anything that will provide status and power to you? Who has time for mass on Sunday when there is football to watch and fantasy football to track?

Clearly, there is a "man-crisis" within the Catholic Church. The New Evangelization will not be successful if Catholic men do not return to the Catholic Church with passion, regularity, and purpose. Few issues are as important as Catholic manhood.

BUILDING A BETTER CATHOLIC MAN

If Catholic men have a hard time believing in God, going to mass, and praying, they will undoubtedly have a hard time considering the priesthood as a viable vocation. The Catholic

---

1   All stats taken from: http://www.newemangelization.com/the-man-crisis-in-the-catholic-church/

man-crisis and the crisis of vocations to the priesthood are intricately linked. You can start building yourself into a better Catholic man by increasing your awareness of the pitfalls of secular manhood and consciously putting into practice a new model of manhood rooted in your relationship with Jesus. To quote Bishop Olmsted again, "Nowhere else can we find the fullness of masculinity as we do in the Son of God."

In our numerous clinical interviews with men applying to the seminary, we typically ask men "what have you learned about being a man?" The men almost always respond in the same way: "I have learned that everything that society has taught me about manhood is false." And they continue by describing a new model of manhood through Jesus—compassion, service-leadership, self-sacrifice, a desire to help others. It is a difficult (probably impossible) model of manhood to achieve here on earth of course, but worthy of sustained effort. The ideal model of Jesus is worth pursuing more so than societal expectations of manhood.

Throughout this book, we have promised to simplify your discernment process. Thinking of manhood and exploring the type of man that you are and want to be can be confusing endeavors without any direction. Let's reset the exploration with a new question for your consideration—**Do you want to live up to secular society's expectations of manhood or do you want to build a foundation of masculinity on Jesus?**

Almost all men who we have interviewed applying to the seminary discuss how their calling to the priesthood emerged from regular mass attendance, deep prayer, and involvement in ministry activities. The first question we routinely ask is "why are you applying to the seminary?" There are a few common themes that we have noticed. First, men do not often know for certain that God is calling them to be a priest. Second, they go to weekly mass, pray, and serve others. And lastly, they cannot quite shake the idea that God wants them to apply to the seminary.

Here is a fundamental belief of our book—being a priest today requires you to be a different kind of man than what society expects of you. Going to mass, praying, and serving others takes on additional meaning. Yes, those are all great spiritual practices that take you deeper into the Catholic faith. While doing so, you are also exhibiting a new kind of manhood. The manhood that your family, community, and Church need from you. The manhood that will help build you into a better man.

LEARNING TO BECOME A SPIRITUAL FATHER

Spending some time thinking about fatherhood is another way to be active in your discernment. You might be saying to yourself right now: priests can't get married and therefore, priests can't be fathers, so why would I think about fatherhood? There are three simple responses to that question. First, priests are fathers. We literally call priests *father*. Second, chances are high that you are already thinking of fatherhood. And three, fatherhood is a big part of manhood.

When men think about fatherhood, they naturally think about the procreative purpose of marriage. Marriage and fatherhood are wonderful vocations. According to Fr. Thomas Berg,

Professor of Moral Theology and Vice Rector and Director of Admissions at St. Joseph's Seminary (Dunwoodie), men should be attracted to marriage and raising a family primarily because those two things require a self-sacrificial love of others. As a seminarian and priest, the focus shifts from biological fatherhood to *spiritual* fatherhood. Most people immediately think that there is a massive difference between the two, but perhaps biological and spiritual fatherhood are more similar than you think. For example, Fr. Jacques Philippe in his book *Interior Freedom* stated that a celibate priest freely chooses to renounce all women while a married man renounces all women except one. A difference of one!

As you think about the priesthood, it is good to think about spiritual fatherhood. Spiritual fatherhood entails being present and engaged with people in ministry, a giving of oneself to the community, and taking responsibility for the care of people in that community. Spiritual fatherhood is not that all different from biological fatherhood, which requires a man to do similar things: be present and engaged with children, give oneself to the family, and take responsibility for the children's well-being. Pope Francis is a good model of spiritual fatherhood. We imagine that Pope Francis sees himself as a spiritual father and he seems to make a point of being present. For example, he has visited several countries, toured multiple prisons, and chosen to live in a more modest apartment that allows him to live in community with others. Perhaps most importantly, he has exhibited an *emotional* presence that communicates a warmth, genuineness, receptivity, and charisma that any father would like to communicate to their child.

TO PARAPHRASE POPE FRANCIS:
ALL OF US, TO BECOME COMPLETE AND MATURE, NEED TO FEEL THE JOY OF FATHERHOOD: EVEN THOSE OF US WHO ARE CELIBATE. FATHERHOOD IS GIVING LIFE TO OTHERS. THIS IS WHY LIVING OUT ONE'S VOCATION TO FATHERHOOD, WHETHER THAT FATHERHOOD IS BOUND UP IN PHYSICAL MARRIAGE OR SPIRITUAL MARRIAGE IN THE PRIESTHOOD, IS ESSENTIAL FOR A MAN TO LIVE OUT THE FULLNESS OF HIS MEANING IN LIFE.

Learning to think and act like a spiritual father is a big part of discerning the priesthood.

SIMPLE AND ACTIVE

Examining your Catholic manhood is the next step to a simple and active approach to discernment.

1. Recognize that society's expectations of manhood are often communicated clearly but learned implicitly by men. Take note. There are other ways to be a man.
2. Answer this primary question—do you want to live up to secular society's expectations of manhood or do you want to build a foundation of masculinity on Jesus?
3. Adopt a view of manhood that is based on Jesus, as the ideal, not secular society's expectations.
4. Consider *spiritual* fatherhood as similar to and equally loving and rewarding as biological fatherhood.

After spending some time in self-reflection and discussion points 1–4, the next step is to engage in some action.

1. Make a list of positive characteristics that you would like to exhibit as a Catholic man.
2. Set a goal to practice one of those characteristics. For example, challenge yourself to show empathy to a friend.
3. Go to mass, pray, engage in service, read Scripture, hang out with other Catholic men with similar goals. Those activities deepen your spirituality AND help to build you into a better Catholic man with greater insights into your vocation.

CHAPTER 6

DEALING WITH
FAMILY AND FRIENDS

We are going to start this chapter with a brief story about John. The story is based on true events involving real people. We changed some of the details to protect the identity of the people involved. Ensuring anonymity is an old (but important) habit of psychologists. Truth be told, John is a composite that represents a lot of men that we have known.

A few years ago, a young man named John decided to apply to the seminary. He heard God's call, wanted to serve, and couldn't deny God's voice any longer. John served in our nation's military and had the stories as well as the physical and mental scars to prove it. Whether it was the military, country, or Church, service was part of who John was and wanted to be.

John was an athletic young man in his mid-20s. It turns out, he was a high school athlete from his hometown, excelling in football and baseball. Straightforward and personable, he had an easy smile and a determined look in his eyes. He was the kind of guy that you wanted to have a beer with at the bar, and you were glad he was sitting next to you. John had a good sense of self-awareness, and he knew who he was. He often said, "I'm not sure I'm supposed to be a priest, but I think people would like a priest like me." We agreed with him.

John was a hero in the military; now he wanted to be a hero in the Church as a priest. He enthusiastically talked about why a vocation to the priesthood appealed to him—coaching youth group sports teams, leading men's retreats, being a military chaplain, and being a spiritual father to many. When our conversation turned to his fears about becoming a priest, the enthusiasm left his voice, and the brightness in his face dimmed. The confident young man who just stared through you with laser focus a moment ago suddenly could not make eye contact. He became fidgety. He hemmed and hawed until he finally said in a low voice, "My parents."

Turns out, John's parents were vehemently against him discerning the priesthood and applying to the seminary. They always envisioned him as a married man, with a large family of his own and grandchildren for them. His parents had his career in business all planned out. In their eyes, he was already a millionaire with a big house and fancy cars. John was a strong man. He was his own man, capable of making difficult decisions. He commanded a unit in the military after all. He was upset about his parents' reaction to his vocational discernment, but submitted his application, got accepted, and entered a seminary.

At this point in the story, we would love to tell you how John is now *Fr.* John at St. Mary's parish, everyone's favorite and beloved pastor. But, he is not. No, John lasted exactly one semester in the seminary. He couldn't withstand the constant negativity from his parents. His discernment came to a breaking point during a holiday vacation, when he returned to his parents' house from the seminary to discover an ex-girlfriend had moved into a spare bedroom at his parents' invitation. Yes, his parents were so against his vocational discernment that they asked an ex-girlfriend to move into their house. The motive was clear—to entice him out of the seminary. And, the ex-girlfriend went along with the plan. John was a great guy, but he was human after all. He fought the good fight, but he didn't stand much of a chance. To us, John is a guy that needlessly "got away."

The sad reality is that there are hundreds, if not thousands, of other men who either did not enter a seminary or left a seminary because their vocations were not supported by family or friends. The particulars of John's story are comparatively rare but highlights the basic point in this chapter. Family and friends can be significant encouragers or discouragers of your vocation. The goal of this chapter is to help you to surround yourself with the encouragers and overcome the discouragers.

THE IMPORTANCE OF ENCOURAGEMENT

Being encouraged by someone or some people is valuable no matter what you do in life. When an actor wins an award, his acceptance speech usually includes thanking everyone that helped him win the award. When an athlete wins a championship, he thanks his coaches, teammates, family, and the fans for their encouragement and support. Nobody gets to where they want to go without other people encouraging and supporting them along the way. This seems to be especially true for the priesthood.

Let's take a look at a couple of statistics. Between 2012–2013, Boston College commissioned a study to answer a perplexing yet straightforward question - what contributes to men entering a seminary and eventually being ordained priests? A little over 1,500 men who were in the seminary or recently ordained completed the research surveys, making it one of the largest research projects of its kind. According to this study, men who had one person encourage them in their discernment were about twice as likely to consider a vocation to the priesthood. The study also found that the more encouragement, the better. There is a cumulative effect. Men who had three persons encourage them were over five times more likely to consider a vocation than someone who wasn't encouraged by anyone!

Earlier in the book, we mentioned some statistics from The Center for Applied Research in the Apostolate (CARA) at Georgetown University. CARA gathers a lot of data on seminarians and priests, making them an excellent source of information on this topic. In 2017, CARA sent surveys to all priests who were just ordained. Not every newly ordained priest responded, but about 444 completed the survey. According to the CARA data, four in five newly ordained priests (82%) reported being encouraged to consider the priesthood by someone in their life. The most frequently-cited encouragers were the parish priest, friend, or another parishioner. On average, they had four people that offered them encouragement and support in their vocation. Discernment and seminary studies can be difficult. There are many reasons to stop discerning, quit the seminary, and lose commitment to the call. Encouragement from others certainly helps.

THE DATA IS VERY CLEAR – ENCOURAGING RELATIONSHIPS ARE A VALUABLE PART OF THE DISCERNMENT PROCESS

WHY IS ENCOURAGEMENT SO IMPORTANT?

To understand the importance of encouragement, we have to look at what encouragement does for men. First, encouragement eliminates many of the problems with discouragement. The challenges that men face when encountering discouragers can be countered by support from encouraging people. Second, receiving encouragement from someone else increases confidence. Hearing a small but persistent call from God to pursue the priesthood can feel strange. A lot of men hear the call from God but lack the confidence to pursue the call. Questions and doubts naturally creep in, which prevent clarity and action. A lack of confidence often leads to avoidance and inaction.

Let's consider an example to highlight this point. Both of us are interested in do-it-yourself (DIY) home improvement projects. It can be fun to work with power tools around the house and save some money by not hiring a professional. We certainly hear the calls from our wives to get things done around the house! But neither of us has received any training in home improvement and we are not very skilled. Thus, when something breaks and needs fixing, we naturally feel less confident with our handyman skills. Procrastination sets in and there seems to be a backlog of projects that need fixing in our houses. We avoid those tasks on the honey-do list because we lack confidence in our own abilities. But, when a more skilled neighbor, friend, or family member come over to help and encourage us, a lot more gets done. We learn from them and our confidence increases.

Encouragement spikes confidence. Confidence leads to directed action. It feels good when you can confidently go in a specific direction. Men who are encouraged can confidently pursue the priesthood without doubt, isolation, or confusion. Encouraged, confident men feel good about the priesthood. Many of the men that we have talked with over the years often cite feeling supported by their parents, roommates, best friends, and other men they know discerning the priesthood. Encouragement from these people in your life can increase your interest, motivation, and resilience during the stresses of the discernment process.

Overall, if you are going through your discernment with encouragement, you are more likely to

✟ have faith: I'm not totally sure, but I will trust that

this is what God wants from me.
- ✟ have clarity: priests are ministerial leaders and spiritual fathers to a faith community.
- ✟ have resolve: this is tough, but I will continue.
- ✟ have positive feelings: I feel excited! I feel purpose!

TO RECAP: ENCOURAGEMENT INCREASE CONFIDENCE, IMPROVES YOUR OUTLOOK, AND STRENGTHENS YOUR MOTIVATION AND RESILIENCE TO OVERCOME CHALLENGES IN DISCERNMENT.

THE PROBLEM WITH DISCOURAGEMENT

Fr. William Leahy, President of Boston College, emphatically stated, "I am convinced there are many young men who are ready to answer the call to priesthood, especially in the United States." We absolutely share that conviction. Yet, how many men do not answer the call to the priesthood because of discouragement? How many Johns are there? We fear that for every John that we know about, there are hundreds if not thousands of other men who were discouraged in similar ways. Those are men who were called to discern the priesthood by God but were discouraged out of discernment by people other than God. That is a tragedy to us and something we want to avoid with you.

We provided some statistics from the Boston College study earlier in the chapter. Here is another statistic—of the men who reported being discouraged from considering the priesthood, the discouragement most likely came from a friend or family member. No doubt, it is extremely difficult to pursue a vocation when a close friend or family member is not supportive. Plus, it is painful to be discouraged by people so close to you. Parents often want their sons to get married, have children, and attain a successful career. Friends might not understand why you would want to be a priest in the first place. There are a wide range of reactions that you might get, from confusion to outright anti-Catholic hostility. None of those reactions provide the support that you need to nourish your vocation.

When you set out in a specific direction on a journey, it is natural to think about the destination. Encouragement makes us think more positively about the destination. However, if you are going through your discernment with discouragement from others, you might

✚   have doubts: is this what God wants from me?

✚   have misconceptions: priests just say mass and sit around the parish.

✚   have misgivings: I don't know. Maybe I shouldn't move forward.

✚   have negative feelings: I feel anxious. I feel alone.

Doubts, misconceptions, misgivings, and negative feelings can cause a negative outlook on the destination of your discernment, i.e., the priesthood. Compare the lists in this chapter—discernment with encouragement versus discernment with discouragement—it is obvious which list nurtures a vocation.

OVERCOMING THE DISCOURAGERS

Family and friends are often the most important people in our lives. It is no wonder why lacking their support and encouragement can be detrimental to a vocation. You simply cannot ignore family and friends when they are discouraging you. Although we often think otherwise, ignoring and avoiding is only a temporary fix. In our experience, we have yet to meet a man who managed to sneak into seminary without his parents, friends, or family members knowing. This section will provide you with some tips that will help you deal with discouraging people. These tips are also helpful if you have not yet experienced discouragement but anticipate a negative response from family and friends.

TIP #1: REVISIT VOCATION WITH AN ADULT IDENTITY

Many developmental psychologists talk about the importance of forming our own identities. Knowing who we are, where we are going, and what we want to do. We start to become more of our own person in adolescence and early adulthood. We reflect on ourselves, our lives, and what we want to accomplish. As you think about your own identity, let's revisit our definition of vocation from Chapter 1. We explained that a vocation from a Catholic perspective is matching your desires with what God desires for you. We believe that people find ultimate happiness and purpose in their lives when they commit to a vocation that integrates their desires and God's desires for them.

Understanding your own desires is part of becoming an adult and part of becoming an adult is owning your vocation. Understanding your own identity and owning your vocation are helpful tools when dealing with discouraging people. You communicate about your calling easier and with more confidence. Men can be more easily influenced by discouraging people when they don't know who they are or what they want. A clear understanding of your own desires provides some protection against discouragers. Moreover, your confidence in yourself will instill confidence in you from others.

TIP #2: SPEAK WITH AN ENCOURAGER

Men are much more likely to enter a seminary and be ordained a priest if they have encouraging people in their lives.

We recommend speaking with a vocation director, priest, youth group leader, or seminarian about your vocation. Their support might make it a little easier for you to have conversations with discouragers. You'll also get some practice talking about your calling. It might feel a little strange in the beginning, but it will slowly become more comfortable. Seminarians and priests are often asked about their calling to the priesthood. As a result, they have a lot of experience talking about their vocation. An added value of talking with a priest or a seminarian is that you can ask them to share their calling story. This will provide you with the opportunity to hear how other men communicate about their vocation. It will give you confidence in your personal story and make you prepared for conversation with discouragers.

As we mentioned earlier, encouragement can change the negative outlook created by discouragement. For example, if a priest encourages you in your vocational discernment, that priest can also clear up misconceptions about the priesthood, share how he overcame his doubts and misgivings, and provide support. Moreover, encouragement from a priest gives you a role model in the vocation that you are discerning. The importance of having such a role model cannot be underestimated. Discerning the priesthood entails doing things that your friends and family might find strange. People often discourage what they do not know and understand. They might scratch their heads in bewilderment because you aren't dating, you haven't applied to graduate school yet, or you haven't ardently pursued some career goal. Similarly, they might get confused when you discuss "religious and spiritual" topics. They are confused because they likely have not gone through such vocational discernment. Talking to a priest gives you the benefit of talking to someone who has gone through what you are going through and can encourage you from that unique perspective.

TIP #3: TALKING WITH OTHERS: START EARLY. DIALOGUE. ANSWER QUESTIONS.

Start Early

It's not always the best strategy to drop the priesthood bomb on an unsuspecting parent or friend with little warning. When you are deciding on a college major, your choice should make sense to those close to you because you have talked about your interests, goals, desires, and plans with them many times. For example, if you select engineering as a major, your family and friends shouldn't be surprised because you have discussed engineering with them several times.

The same is true for talking about discerning the priesthood. Speak early and often with your family and friends about your religious involvement and service. Let them know that you are working hard to understand what God wants for you in your life. The earlier you start this process, the better. The idea here is that you are keeping people in the loop. It will be less shocking and controversial if you eventually decide to enter seminary because your choice seems like the next logical step. People in your life will be hard-pressed to offer discouragement when you have familiarized them to the idea of the priesthood and it makes sense to them.

Dialogue

As you gradually discuss your calling with others, it is essential that share some of the reasons why you believe God might be calling you to the priesthood. Tell them about your calling story, your personal desires, and how you think those desires might be fulfilled in the priesthood. This type of sharing shows discouragers that you are serious about your vocation. It also shows them that you are thoughtful, reflective, and have good reasons to believe that God might be calling you to the priesthood.

Open up the dialogue by inviting others to share their thoughts, concerns, or questions. The idea here is to give your friends or family the opportunity to voice their perspective or ask any questions. By opening up the dialogue, you are showing respect for them and an openness to their thoughts. People are going to have different reactions. Some people might resort to discouraging you and others might offer you support. However, people will be less discouraging if you are the one to invite their thoughts and questions.

Clarify

Many people are unfamiliar with the discernment process and never met someone who is thinking about becoming a priest. You can clarify their confusion by answering questions and helping them to understand what you are pursuing. You are going to want to address their questions openly and honestly. You might not have all of the answers either. A useful resource is this FAQ section from the Pittsburgh Diocese webpage about vocations: http://pghpriest.com/faq/ There are short video clips from our very own Fr. Joseph Freedy, who wrote this book's foreword. Sharing, dialoguing, and clarifying misconceptions is one of the best ways to win support, prevent discouragement, and receive the type of encouragement that will last through your seminary years.

TIP #4: ACCEPT THAT SOME PEOPLE WILL REMAIN DISCOURAGERS

Even if you implement these tips to perfection, some people in your life might remain discouragers. After sharing, dialoguing, and clarifying in an open and honest way, sometimes we have to accept the fact that not everyone is going to be on board. Change is always possible, but some people take more time. That is why tip #1 is important. You need to know where you stand in your vocation. It is much easier to accept that some people are not going to support you if you have confidence in God's desire for you and you understand your own desires. There is good news though: many of the discouragers that men face early on in their discernment eventually come around.

SIMPLE AND ACTIVE

Seeking encouragement is the next step to a simple and active approach to discernment.

1. Identify a priest who you can talk to about your sense of calling. A priest has gone through what you are going through can be a great role model.
2. Recognize those family members and friends in your life who are supportive and encouraging of you. Spend more time with them!
3. Rely on the support and encouragement from other priests, family members, and friends to overcome challenges in the discernment process and remain trusting and resolute.

After spending some time identifying and connecting with sources of encouragement, the next step is to overcome the discouragers.

1. Identify people in your life (e.g., family members and friends) who have discouraged your discernment.
2. Actively seek to overcome their discouragement through sharing, dialoguing, and clarifying.
3. Don't let their discouragement damage your calling.

CHAPTER 7

I'm Not Worthy Enough to be a Priest

W̲e gave a talk at a vocations retreat for high school guys who were thinking about entering the seminary after they graduated last year. For this particular talk, we started by asking the young men, "How many of you feel *worthy* to be a priest?" In scanning the room, we noticed that nobody had their hand raised. To our surprise, the vocations director who was running the retreat also did not have his hand raised. Yes, even an ordained priest didn't think that he was worthy to be a priest. It quickly became clear to us that unworthiness is a significant barrier that many, if not all, men face in their discernment of the priesthood. Even priests who are already ordained struggle with their unworthiness. The purpose of this chapter is to shine a light on the common, but rarely discussed, topic of unworthiness among men discerning the priesthood.

We know that many discerning men, seminarians, and priests consider themselves unworthy. To counter this widespread feeling of unworthiness, we'd love to spend the rest of this chapter telling you about how worthy you are of being ordained to the priesthood. We want to affirm you in your vocation and encourage you. After all, we just talked about the value of encouragement in the last chapter. Unfortunately, simply trying to convince you of your worthiness would be doing you and your vocation a disservice. When it comes to your vocation, it is not a matter of if you earned it or not.

AN UNEARNED PROMOTION

A good starting point in our discussion of worthiness is this basic principle—your vocation is a gift from God. It is given to you freely, but it is not because you are deserving, or you earned a vocation. People are imperfect. We make mistakes. We fail to uphold our responsibilities. We sin. Our imperfections drive us away from God and make us feel less worthy of his gifts. Our mistakes set the stage for both our undeservedness and for God to give us the gift of a vocation. It is a wonderful paradox. Contrast that wonderful paradox with a typical situation in the workplace. Let's say that you messed up an important project at work. You would likely be fired, demoted, or sternly corrected by your boss. That's not how God works with vocations. Mistakes and shortcomings do not automatically disqualify you from living out your vocation. Once God gives us our vocation, then our free will kicks in. We can voluntary choose to take actions that nurture the gift, or we can act in ways that prevent us from fully accepting that gift.

If you start with the principle that your vocation is a free gift that God gives you, then you can understand why many men feel unworthy of this gift. God's gifts are given freely and undeservedly. As a result, nobody is perfectly worthy of their vocation. It is okay to feel unworthy of a calling to the priesthood. The feeling of unworthiness is accurate. It is accurate to feel unworthy after you are given an awesome gift that you did not earn. The challenge is not in knowing if you are worthy or not; the challenge is in rising above your sense of unworthiness to pursue God's will in your life.

COMMON SOURCES OF UNWORTHINESS

I'm not prepared.

It's important to understand that the high school guys at our talk had not gone through the seminary yet. Seminary is training to become a priest. They were not trained, prepared, or ready to take on the responsibilities of the priesthood. Of course, no man is prepared for the priesthood unless he has gone through the appropriate training. Over the course of several years, seminarians learn the theology of the Church, how to run a parish, and how to administer the sacraments. If you are reading this book, then there is a good chance that you have not had the opportunity to receive all of the training and preparation that the seminary provides. It is easy to understand why guys might feel unworthy of the priesthood if they have not been prepared through the seminary training. A lack of preparation and training is a common source of feeling unworthy. As a result, men say to themselves "I'm not prepared to be a priest" and stop their active discernment of the priesthood.

I'm not holy enough.

The priesthood is inherently religious and spiritual. Priests are leaders within the Catholic Church. They pray and help others engage in prayer and the sacraments. Priests strive to live a holy life and their job is to nourish holiness in others. Some men look at priests and the religious and spiritual nature of the priesthood and say to themselves, "I am not a saint. I can't be a priest." Their feelings of unworthiness are tied to a deep sense of spiritual inadequacy and they do not think that they will ever be "holy enough" to be ordained a priest. Some men have an unrealistic expectation for themselves and their personal holiness. They might see priests as perfect people who never make mistakes and live incredibly holy lives 24/7. We have heard men say, "I'm not a holy roller. I'll never be a good priest." Their inability to live up to these overly-lofty and unrealistic expectations can cause feelings of unworthiness and bring discernment to a screeching halt.

My sins are too great.

Believing that you are too sinful to be a priest is another main source of unworthiness. It is closely tied to the idea of not being holy enough to be a priest. Some men dwell on their past mistakes. They are unable to move on. Men are notorious for lingering in regret, guilt, and shame. Their fixation on their own shortcomings keeps them stuck in the past and unable to see the future. They might have deep feelings of sadness about what they have done in their lives and say, "I'm too sinful to be a priest. The priesthood is not for me." As we mentioned earlier, we have all made mistakes and have areas for growth. There is some legitimacy to feelings of guilt or regret, and they can actually be helpful at times. Guilt and regret can drive motivation to positive change. On the other hand, growth is stunted when men are overcome with feelings of shame. Shame worsens feelings of unworthiness to accept God's gifts to us, such as a vocation.

By describing those common sources, we are trying to make it clear that there are good reasons for you to feel some unworthiness. However, these reasons and your sense of unworthiness should not be a barrier to pursuing the priesthood.

AN ANTIDOTE TO UNWORTHINESS

I can become prepared.

Earlier in the book, we talked about our own journey to becoming psychologists. We had to spend five years in graduate school studying psychology, learning how to counsel people, and getting all the necessary clinical training. When we started graduate school, we doubted our ability to treat effectively bullied children, depressed teenagers, anxious college students, and traumatized soldiers returning from deployment. We felt unworthy to step into a therapeutic relationship and help a suffering patient. Doubting questions and feelings of unworthiness plagued our mind. Truth be told, we *were not* worthy or ready.

The story did not end there. We did not throw in the towel because we were not effective counselors on the first day of graduate school. We had to work hard, study, learn skills, and develop ourselves into people that were capable of taking on the responsibilities of our profession. We had to acquire the necessary training and preparation. Despite our reservations, our unworthiness did not stop us from pursuing what we believe God desired for us in our lives.

All of the seminaries in the world would be empty if men like you did not apply because they felt unworthy to be a priest. Indeed, you are not ready to be a priest today unless you have completed all of the training and the Church declares your worthiness at ordination. No one is ready for ordination on the first day of seminary. As we mentioned earlier in the book, the good news is that the Church discerns your vocation with you. And the Church goes a step further by providing you with the training that you need to become a priest worthy of serving the people in the Church. That is the entire purpose of the seminary: to train you to become a man worthy of the priesthood. At the ordination mass for men to become priests, the bishop or cardinal actually says to the entire congregation that you are "worthy" to be a priest. The power of such a declaration is immense and its impact is tangible. Allow God, through His Church, the opportunity to help you grow in worthiness as you receive the needed preparation and training.

I can overcome my mistakes.

The history of the Church is loaded with men who seem to be the most unworthy and unlikely people to become ordained priests. Before St. Paul was struck with a heavenly light and converted to Christianity, he harshly persecuted the early Christians. St. Paul eventually became one of the most influential priests and bishops of the early Church. St. Augustine detailed his own questionable past in his famous book *Confessions.* He fell into lust, dabbled with heresy, stole from his neighbor, and had a son before he was married. St. Augustine went on to become a priest, bishop, saint, and Doctor of the Church.

In more recent times, a story broke on the news that surprised many people. After the annual Lenten penance service at the Vatican, Pope Francis walked across the marble floor of Saint Peter's Basilica and headed toward the confessional. The men and women at the Lenten service expected Pope Francis to step into the confessional and to hear confessions. However, the confessional was already occupied by another priest. Soon it became clear that Pope Francis was not walking to the confessional to hear confessions for others, but to confess his own sins. He knelt down and offered his confession while people watched in shock. The story made headlines in major news outlet. Yet, there is nothing newsworthy about confessing sins because everyone has sins to confess. Yes, even the Pope has sins to confess too.

The purpose of highlighting the lives of St. Paul, St. Augustine, and Pope Francis is not to give you a license to "sin and sin boldly" as the phrase commonly goes. If you have a history of killing Christians, there is a good chance you will not get accepted into seminary. Rather, their stories shine a light on a reality that is often overlooked by men who do not believe they are holy enough to be a priest. Priests are human beings. Yes, they commit their lives to spiritual growth and holiness. Yes, they are spiritual leaders in the community. Yes, they are fundamentally good. But we cannot forget that they are also inclined to make mistakes like everyone else. After all, even the Pope goes to confession. Rumor has it he goes every two weeks.

I am worthy to get help.

Although you might not be perfectly prepared, trained, and worthy to be a priest today, you are worthy of transforming yourself into a better man. We want to encourage you to reflect on some of the behaviors that make you feel unworthy, guilty, or regretful. This will provide you with a starting point for the areas that you can grow and receive help. Some personality weaknesses and mistakes are more significant and indicative of psychological concerns. In such circumstances, an appropriate active step to take in your discernment is to seek help from a mental health professional. We have referred several men to counseling over the years. Counseling not only helps to alleviate psychological concerns, but clarifies questions and confusion in discernment because you learn to think more clearly. Here is a brief list of issues from the United States Conference of Catholic Bishops that would warrant seeking professional help in the context of vocational discernment:

- ☦ Substance or alcohol abuse
- ☦ Addictions
- ☦ Pornography use
- ☦ Sexual immaturity
- ☦ Severe psychological disorders
- ☦ Obesity
- ☦ Intense feelings of shame

✠   Difficulty receiving and implementing feedback

Psychological counseling is one of the most researched health interventions across the health and medical professions. You might be surprised to hear that in some seminary programs nearly 90% of the men receive brief, growth-oriented individual counseling at some point in their formation. Counseling can reduce distress, increases quality of life, improve work, academic, and social functioning, and leads to better physical health. It is common sense—if you have a problem, seek the appropriate help to address the problem.

I am worthy of transformation.

St. Paul, St. Augustine, and Pope Francis all used their own sense of unworthiness as a way to transform themselves. God is limitless in the ways he can inspire, forgive, and redeem. Your own sense of unworthiness can be an excellent way for you to become more aware of the ways you need to grow. There are many legitimate ways that you can grow so as to present a worthier version of yourself to God. St. Paul realized the horrible acts he committed and was pushed to a deep conversion. St. Augustine's sinfulness was a motivating force in his pursuit of holiness. Pope Francis recognized the need to teach others through his actions and not just his words. These examples highlight an essential point: your unworthiness can point you in the right direction.

SIMPLE AND ACTIVE

1. Embrace the idea that feeling unworthy is a common and accurate feeling that can lead to positive growth.
2. It is important to understand the common sources of unworthiness to simplify your discernment.
    ✠   You may feel unworthy of a call to the priesthood

because of a lack of preparation, unrealistic expectations of yourself, and focusing too much on your sins.

✝   In some instances, your sense of unworthiness is rooted in a deeper psychological issue or personality weakness. You should take the active step of seeking help from a mental health professional in those circumstances.

3.   Your discernment can become more active when you prepare appropriately, seek the necessary support, work to overcome your mistakes, and engage in a transformative process to become a better man.

CHAPTER 8

DATING AND MARRIAGE

W e are both happily married men. We love our wives and our children. God called us to the vocation of marriage and we are doing our best to live out that vocation. We start with that disclaimer of sorts because we want to be clear about our positive experiences as married men and because our wives will likely read this chapter! This chapter is going to describe some tough realities of marriage. Our description of the realities is meant to present a more authentic perspective on married life. We are doing so because men often rule out the priesthood because of unrealistic expectations, misconceptions, and idealized perspectives of marriage.

Those unrealistic expectations, misconceptions, and idealized perspectives become a significant barrier to discerning the priesthood freely. Yes, marriage is a wonderful vocation and has brought us and many other men much joy. However, marriage does not guarantee a life of pleasure and bliss. Marriage is not a vocation free from pains and challenges. In fact, some priests have told us that they think marriage is a harder vocation than the priesthood. If you are called to marriage, we want you to follow that calling. We do not want you to become a priest if you are supposed to get married. That would not work. If you eventually discover that you are called to marriage, by reading this chapter you will at least have a better understanding of marriage from two happily married

Catholic guys.

A THOUGHT EXPERIMENT

Take a moment and allow us to walk you through a thought experiment. Imagine a young, vibrant Catholic couple. They are recently engaged, brimming with smiles, and have begun planning the wedding. Within the hustle and bustle of planning a wedding while leading busy lives early in their professional careers, they sign up for marriage preparation classes at their local parish. They go to the first class with the parish priest and begin telling the priest about their relationship, lives, hopes, and dreams as a married couple.

After listening to their story for a while, the priest finally has something to say. The priest turns to the man and says, "You know what you need right now? You need more seminary experience before you get married."

Sounds crazy right? We have never heard of a priest actually saying that to an engaged man. We imagine that the wife-to-be would take great offense if a priest offered such a suggestion to her husband-to-be. But what if a priest actually said that? It is an intriguing question.

Now, let's draw the parallel to men discerning the priesthood. Men who think that they are being called to the priesthood are often cautioned by some well-intentioned family members, priests, and friends that they should put off considering the priesthood until they get more dating experience. Similarly, men are advised to wait on committing to the priesthood until they are sure that they have not found "the one." In other words, when a man talks to a trusted person in his life about considering the priesthood, he is often told, "You know what you need right now? You need more dating experience before you go into a seminary to discern the priesthood."

To be clear, there is nothing wrong with dating women.

Some men probably do need dating experience to grow in maturity, gain life experience, and to explore marriage as a possible vocation. That is the key—you date *when you feel called to marriage*.

The problem is that hundreds and thousands of men have been advised to date when they were feeling called to the priesthood. Dating when you feel called to the priesthood clouds and confuses discernment just how going into a seminary would be very strange when you are planning a wedding.

Why get on the train to Texas when you are supposed to go to Michigan?

MEN REACT SIMILARLY TO CELIBACY AND VEGETABLES

Think back to your dinner table as a child. We bet you grimaced when your parents gave you a scoop of vegetables. "Vegetables, yuck!" you moaned. We see the same reaction from men when we talk about celibacy in the priesthood. "Celibacy, yuck! Not on my plate." Most men react negatively without knowing the full meaning and purpose of celibacy. The reason that celibacy elicits such negative reactions is that most men think of celibacy from a standpoint of what they cannot do. The immediate first thought is often, "Celibacy means that I can't have sex." Inside the mind of most men is this basic logic: *I want to marry, have sex, and father children. Priests cannot get married, have sex, or father children. I do not want to become a priest because priests cannot marry, have sex, or father children.* The very thought of celibacy can be a deal breaker for men and they immediately rule out the priesthood.

A basic definition of celibacy is that it is a discipline that priests assume, which prevents them from getting married. The natural question to ask is—are there *any* benefits to celibacy? We are not theologians or scripture scholars, but we can offer an obvious answer to that question. Jesus was celibate. Priests are ordained to act *in persona Christi,* which is Latin for "in the person of Christ." They embody the "person of Christ" all the way down to Jesus's sexuality by embracing the discipline of celibacy. Jesus sacrificed for all of us. Celibacy is one way that priests sacrifice for others. Also, practically speaking, celibacy enables a priest to be more available to his parish.

Our society is overly sexualized, which can distort people's views of celibacy. As a result, celibacy is seen as an unhealthy relic of the past that should be dispensed with. Celibacy is often blamed whenever anything goes wrong in the priesthood. If a news headline read, "Catholic priest twists an ankle while walking to car in parking lot," you can bet someone will blame the injury on celibacy. The prevalence of this anti-celibacy bias in our society prompted Fr. Harrison Ayre to start a Twitter hashtag #celibacymatters to speak more vocally about the positives of celibacy.

Acknowledging some benefits of celibacy can help you move forward in your discernment.

Beneath the surface of the sexual act is a deeper desire for intimacy and interpersonal connection. Men often lack the words to articulate their deeper desires, but we have talked with men about their fears of being lonely as a priest and lacking someone to come home to at night. Those fears are legitimate. Taken together, the lack of sex and perceived loneliness of a priestly lifestyle are significant barriers for men considering the priesthood. To men experiencing those fears, marriage seems like a natural solution to both problems.

We have talked to priests about their sense of loneliness and social support. The consistent message we heard back is that priests can be as lonely or as socially connected as they want to be and celibacy is a key factor. Priests can use celibacy as an excuse to be lonely or use celibacy to connect with as many people as possible in ministry, service, fellowship, friendship, and support. Yes, celibacy is sacrificial, but people often forget that it enhances a priest's ability to love and connect with others. Celibacy allows you, as a priest, to say "yes" to loving more people. Rather than only viewing celibacy from a restrictive perspective (i.e., what I can't do), begin to consider how celibacy opens up possibilities. Celibacy enables priests to serve God and others more easily with an undivided heart.

IDEAL VERSUS REAL: MARRIAGE AND FATHERHOOD

Here are a few excerpts from the Catechism of the Catholic Church about marriage:

✚ The intimate community of life and love which constitutes the married state has been established by the Creator.

✚ The greatness of the matrimonial union exists in all cultures.

✚ Since God created man and woman, their mutual love becomes an image of the absolute and unfailing love with which God loves man.

To sum up, Catholic marriage was established by the Creator, is great in all cultures, and is an image of God's infinite love for us. All of those excerpts are 100% true and grounded in sound Catholic theology. Those excerpts also have a way of describing marriage that may gloss over some of the grittier realities of the lived experience of married couples. There is nothing about marital stress, conflicting personalities, financial pressures, and in-laws in those excerpts.

Social science research has tracked the marital satisfaction of couples over long periods of time. The general finding is what many psychologists and marriage counselors refer to as "The U Curve." Married couples are at their peak happiness one to three years after they are married; this period is commonly referred to as the honeymoon stage. You are young, carefree, high on life. After the honeymoon stage, there is a prolonged period of decreased marital satisfaction. This period is marked by career pressures, financial strain, parenting stress. Couples "bottom out" on this part of the U Curve until around the ages 45–55. Once career and financial stability has been achieved and children are launched into adulthood, there is less stress. The other side of the U is an upswing in marital satisfaction into your 50s, 60s, and 70s. We often forget about that long period of decreased marital happiness, but it is real and challenging for married couples.

Marriage has both unitive and procreative functions. Lots of people automatically think that the Catholic Church can be prudish when it comes to sexual activity. However, that is not necessarily true. The Church encourages married couples to engage in sexual activity to unify and strengthen their bond. Unmarried Catholic men often develop an idealized image of this unitive function in marriage. They tend to equate marriage with unlimited, unbridled sexual activity. We have heard men say, "*I get to have sex anytime I want when I get married.*" You may be thinking something similar. The added bonus to sex within marriage is that men avoid the sin of having sex outside of marriage. Who does not want unlimited, sinless sexual activity for the rest of their lives? It almost sounds too good to be true, doesn't it? We have learned in life that when something seems too good to be true, most of the time it is. When we hear men discuss their unrealistic expectations of marriage, we are reminded of some advice we received while preparing for marriage. It is called the "95/5 advice"; 5% of marriage is about sexual activity with your spouse and 95%

of marriage is about all the other stuff.

Procreation is a strange word to lots of people. Basically, it means that marriage is geared toward producing and raising children. For a second, think of becoming a father. There is an old but prevailing model of fatherhood that needs addressed. The old model of fatherhood is that the father in the family works 9am – 5pm, comes home, and is greeted at the door by his wife, and a hot dinner that is just about finished baking in the oven. While waiting for dinner to be served, the father retires to the living room to read the paper quietly while the children are setting the table or playing outside in the sundrenched neighborhood. That model *may* have existed for *some* fathers and families many, many years ago. Perhaps that model only truly existed in Norman Rockwell paintings. We are sorry to say, but we do not know any fathers that actually live that way now.

Studies have been done with thousands of fathers over the past ten years to understand better how fathers are involved in their families in the twenty-first century. A new model of fatherhood has emerged. Fathers are spending more time with their children than previous generations and are involved in their children's lives in more versatile ways. The Modern Dad does more than work and come home to read the newspaper. He changes diapers, helps with homework, drives children to activities, coach sports teams, wards off scary monsters underneath the bed, goes to the doctor's office, nurtures, hugs, and kisses his children—just to name a few activities. A 2016 study out of Boston College's Center for Work and Family summed up the Modern Dad by saying that they are involved, caring, but conflicted. It is difficult to try to do everything and "have it all."

MARRIAGE AND FATHERHOOD *SHOULD* BE ATTRACTIVE

We do not want to be inconsistent in our message to you. These topics are complex and thought-provoking. That is one of the reasons why we have offered ways to simplify your discernment throughout this book. With that in mind, bear with us as we return to a theme about marriage and fatherhood from the Masculinity Chapter.

In the Masculinity Chapter, we provided a quote from Fr. Thomas Berg that emphasized how men should be attracted to marriage and fatherhood when they are discerning a call to the priesthood. We agree with Fr. Berg and for good reason. The themes that attract men to the married life overlap with the themes that attract men to the priesthood. Take a step back and ponder some of the common denominators of attractiveness between marriage and the priesthood. Both require the following:

- ✟ self-sacrificial love of others
- ✟ developing and maintaining intimate connections with people
- ✟ responsibility to other people beyond yourself
- ✟ engagement in the daily care and concern of others
- ✟ accessibility to be present and available to help others
- ✟ 100% commitment that needs renewal each day
- ✟ assuming a fathering role to others
- ✟ long hours, difficult decisions, personal challenges, and relationship difficulties

Self-sacrificial love for others is at the top of the list. You will exhibit self-sacrificial love for others as a biological and spiritual father. The bottom line is that if you are attracted to marrying a woman and becoming a biological father, then you are attracted to the same things as a priest because you essentially commit your undivided heart to the Church and become a spiritual father to many. Recall what we wrote in the masculinity chapter. As a seminarian and priest, the focus of the role shifts from biological fatherhood to *spiritual* fatherhood. A celibate priest freely chooses to renounce all women while a married man renounces all women except one. A difference of one!

The qualities of a good father are similar whether you are considering marriage or priesthood. Fr. Berg put it another way, which is worth thinking about: if you cannot see yourself as a good husband and father, then it will be difficult to be a good priest. The late Fr. Michael Scanlan, the former President of Franciscan University of Steubenville, is a great example. "Fr. Mike," as he was affectionately called, was university president from 1974–2000 and recently died in 2017. Before he became a priest, Fr. Mike went to Harvard Law School and was a lawyer in the U.S. Judge Advocate Corps of the Air Force. Everyone would have expected him to marry a beautiful woman and to have a large Catholic family. In fact, he was engaged to be married to such a woman. He obviously became a priest and did not marry and have biological children. However, that did not stop people from considering him a spiritual father. In fact, there is a tribute video of him, which was made after his passing, entitled "A Father to Us All": https://vimeo.com/216954806

The priesthood is not for men avoiding intimate, interpersonal relationships or who are anxious and awkward around women. The priesthood is not for men who prefer independence, a "bachelor's lifestyle," and freedom from children. The priesthood is not for men who want to escape the messiness of people's lives. The exact opposite is true. The priesthood is for men who deeply love others and people look to as a father figure. The priesthood is for men who are attracted to married life but choose to embrace celibacy. They choose celibacy because it draws them closer to God, the people they serve, and the Church. They sacrifice the good that comes from marriage for the good that comes from the priesthood.

Marriage and the priesthood are two beautiful and fulfilling vocations. The type of man who would make a holy priest is the same type of man who would make an excellent father and husband. We hope that you are able to see both the beauty and challenge of each vocation. Marriage is not without struggle, sacrifice, and hard-work. The same can be said of the priesthood. Ultimately, you are going to find the greatest happiness in pursuing God's calling for your, whether it is as a married man, single man, or a priest. If you believe that God might be calling you to the priesthood, do not let an over-romanticized idea of marriage or irrational fears of celibacy get in the way of your discernment. As we mentioned earlier, our sex-focused culture does not make it easy. However, we also know that celibacy enables men to love many people, commit to their ministry, and deepen their relationship with God. Celibate priests are more easily able to serve God and others with an undivided heart.

SIMPLE AND ACTIVE

1. Do not date if you feel a calling to the priesthood, as dating can confuse your discernment. Rather, commit to the possibility of the priesthood by engaging in activities that are congruent with the vocation of the priesthood.

2. Reflect on celibacy and list three benefits of living out a celibate priesthood:

    a_____
    b_____
    c_____

3. Do not over-romanticize and idealize marriage and bio-

logical fatherhood.

4.   Identify qualities that would make you a good *spiritual father* to many people.

5.   Marriage and the priesthood are distinct vocations in the Catholic Church. One is not better than the other. The best route in discernment is to pursue actively the vocation that you believe God is calling you to.

CHAPTER 9

YOUR STRENGTHS CAN
SERVE THE CHURCH

✟ Early humans use their problem-solving skills and intelligence to create and control fire.

✟ Michelangelo crafts the Sistine Chapel with his artistic skills.

✟ Philip Rivers throws for 50,000 yards and 342 touchdowns as the QB for San Diego Chargers.

✟ Stephen Colbert and Jim Gaffigan make millions of people laugh on a nightly basis.

Throughout history, men have accomplished some truly amazing feats. We have invented cars, airplanes, rockets, and Mars rovers. We figured out how to transport clean water into our homes and light those homes by harnessing the power of electricity. We have cured chronic diseases, developed vaccines, and walked on the moon. Without a doubt, mankind has pushed the present forward into a future that would have baffled our ancestors. These accomplishments are no small feat. They required patience, endurance, visionary minds, hard-work, study, and practical know-how, among many other talents and skills.

The most celebrated accomplishments in the history of mankind are the result of people putting their strengths, skills, and talents into practice. Men found their passions, understood what they were good at, and were able to revolutionize the world around them. They created success in their lives by using their strengths to accomplish their goals. That is what we will talk about in this chapter. We want to help you come to understand your strengths. God gave you strengths and He wants you to use those strengths in your vocation. God gives everyone gifts. It is our responsibility to recognize these gifts in ourselves and figure out how we can use them to serve God and his Church.

STRENGTHS ARE BUZZING

You may have noticed that strengths are all the buzz right now. If you scroll through your Facebook newsfeed, you will probably find a few links to tests or articles that claim to tell you about your strengths. They usually have some catchy titles like, "These 5 Strengths Changed My LIFE!" or "Find Out Your BEST Traits FREE." Strengths have become a hot topic in the popular media. Part of the reason for the emphasis on strengths lately is because the field of psychology went through a bit of a transformation.

Psychologists used to focus mostly on what went wrong with people. They studied mental illness, impairment, dysfunction, pathology, deficits. In recent times, psychologists decided that they should also study what goes right with people. The language is a little bit different—virtue, happiness, flourishing, success, and strengths. There is a whole field of psychology that focuses exclusively on studying the "positive" side of human behavior. This field is known as "Positive Psychology," and it has gained a lot of traction over the last few years. Positive psychology flips the script to help people identify what they do right and what they are good at.

Rather than leaving you to Buzzfeed or Facebook, we wanted to help you understand your strengths in a way that is informed by this new field of positive psychology. And more importantly, we want to help you understand how your strengths can tie into your vocational calling.

WHEN WE TALK ABOUT STRENGTHS, WE ARE REFERRING TO YOUR TALENTS, SKILLS, OR PERSONALITY TRAITS. YOUR STRENGTHS ARE THE THINGS THAT YOU CONSISTENTLY DO WELL AND ARE CONSIDERED POSITIVE AND HEALTHY.

For example, if you consistently turn in assignments late in class, we would not consider your tardiness to be a strength. But, if you study a lot and do well in school, we would consider your academic ability to be a strength. Your strengths will often be recognized or complimented on by your coaches, teachers, family members, or friends. You may be known as a stellar basketball player, a hard worker, excellent writer, or "natural born leader." You may be the type of person who has a knack for motivating people, giving speeches, or having deep one-on-one conversations. These are all personal strengths. They are your talents, skills, or personality traits that you can put into practice.

STRENGTHS ENLIVEN LIFE

Psychological literature tells us that people feel more positive emotions when they use their strengths. For example, people feel a greater sense of meaning or purpose in their lives. They are enlivened, energized, and motivated. You might be familiar with Stephen Colbert, the writer, comedian, and talk show host of *The Late Show*. Colbert is well-known for his comedic bits, political commentary, and communication skills. He uses his strengths of creativity, humor, and communication to bring laughter to his viewers. He challenges them to think more critically about the world around them and raises their awareness of issues in society. Colbert's use of his strengths provides him with a greater sense of meaning and purpose in his life because it enables him to accomplish his vocational goals.

Psychological studies have also found that when people use their strengths, it increases their well-being and leads to a happier life. To think about this more simply, it feels good to do what you are good at. You have probably had an experience in your life where you did something well and it gave you a healthy sense of pride and confidence. A teacher, parent, friend, or coach may have complimented you on a "job well done." These sorts of experiences push us forward and make us feel better about ourselves and our life choices. When you reflect on your strengths, it can be helpful to ask, "What skills, talents, or traits do I have that make me feel enlivened or motivated when I put them into practice?"

STRENGTHS IN THE PRIESTHOOD

Who comes to mind when you think of priests that have used their strengths to serve God? Bishop Robert Barron is probably at the top of many lists. He has close to 137,000 subscribers on YouTube and his regular videos on timely topics are viewed by millions. Bishop Barron used his academic knowledge, communication skills, and understanding of modern media to create the *Word on Fire Catholic Ministries* and *The Catholicism Project*. Bishop Barron identified his unique strengths and put them to use. Not every priest is going to be the next Bishop Barron. In fact, most priests are never going to create a successful TV series, YouTube videos, or give interviews for the nightly news. Though the great preachers and public figures of the Church tend to get the most attention, there are many different types of roles in the priesthood that require an entirely different set of skills.

One of the common things we hear in our work with men who are discerning the priesthood is that they fear not having the right strengths to be a good priest. For example, one of the biggest themes we noticed was that many guys are afraid of having to deliver a homily in front of a group of people at mass. There is a myth that to be a good priest, you must be extroverted and charismatic, a gregarious leader, and polished speaker. The mythological good priest wows his congregation with his preaching and earns rounds of applause after every homily. Men who buy into this myth typically say to themselves, "Oh man. I would NOT be good at public speaking," or, "I really don't like being the center of attention." Their fear of not having a particular strength makes them more hesitant to discern the priesthood.

Lots of people fear public speaking. Yes, the fear of not being able to preach a great homily is real. However, focusing purely on weakness can cause you to become a little short-sighted and narrow-minded. We want you to improve your weaknesses, whatever they may be. But, we also want you to emphasize your skills and abilities. Perhaps you do much better in one-on-one conversations, or you're a good listener. This type of man might not be known for his energetic and captivating Sunday sermons, but he will likely have a knack for hearing confessions, providing one-on-one spiritual guidance, or lending support to a fellow priest and parishioner.

The Church needs men with diverse strengths to serve a diversity of people.

A THOUGHT EXPERIMENT

Think of your favorite priest who has had a positive impact on you. What makes this priest your favorite? What characteristics does he have that make him a good priest? Chances are, there are many different reasons he is your favorite. He might be deeply spiritual, patient, a good confessor, a strong preacher, down to earth, athletic, funny, good at listening, or creative. If we took one hundred people and asked them to list the characteristics they appreciate most in their favorite priest, we would probably come up with nearly one hundred different traits. There is no one size fits all when it comes to the priesthood. Each man has his own skills, talents, and personality.

If you eventually decide to go into the seminary and are required to study Latin, you will probably hear an old story about St. John Vianney. John Vianney was not known for his language abilities. He struggled to learn Latin and had a hard time grasping lofty theological ideas. He worked hard to make it through his seminary studies, though he was not the sharpest tool in the shed. St. Vianney could have easily focused on his weaknesses and given up on his pursuit of the priesthood. Instead, he capitalized on his perseverance and deep spiritual connection to God. This strength shone brightly in his ministry. He was known for spending over ten hours a day in the confessional. He preached in a way that was simple and clear, which appealed to his uneducated community. Simply put, St. John Vianney effectively used his strengths in his ministry.

Sometimes when men get so focused on what they cannot do, they forget about the skills and talents they bring to the table. The reality is that the Church needs men that have their own set of strengths. The Church needs men who have strong administrative skills to run parishes, good listeners to hear confessions, communicators to preach the word of God, and teachers to educate the faithful. The list goes on. The question is not whether you have the *right* strengths to be a priest, but how will you use *your* strengths as a priest to serve the Church.

NAMING YOUR STRENGTHS TO HELP YOUR DISCERNMENT

One of the things that we promised you at the start of this book was to make your discernment more active. Your discernment can become more active by identifying your strengths and how you can use them to serve the Church. This section is formatted in a workbook style and will include a little homework for you. Follow the directions.

1. We created a list to help you start thinking about your own strengths. The directions are simple. Review the list and check all that apply to you. Remember, a strength is something that you do consistently well that is positiveand healthy.

- ☐ Singing
- ☐ Storytelling
- ☐ Drawing
- ☐ Mentoring
- ☐ Counseling
- ☐ Acting
- ☐ Writing
- ☐ Technology
- ☐ Sports, athletics
- ☐ Teaching
- ☐ Preaching
- ☐ Organization and coordination
- ☐ Music
- ☐ Social intelligence
- ☐ Teamwork
- ☐ Fairness
- ☐ Leadership
- ☐ Prudence
- ☐ Self-Regulation
- ☐ Appreciation of beauty and excellence
- ☐ Gratitude
- ☐ Hope
- ☐ Managing a team
- ☐ Energy and stamina
- ☐ Youth Ministry
- ☐ Young Adult Ministry
- ☐ Adult Ministry
- ☐ Landscaping and gardening
- ☐ Strategy and analysis
- ☐ Public speaking
- ☐ Web design
- ☐ Humility
- ☐ Illustration

❑ Forgiveness
❑ Photography
❑ Videography
❑ Playing an instrument
❑ Research
❑ Mechanical work
❑ Administration
❑ Communication
❑ Creativity
❑ Curiosity
❑ Grit
❑ Love of learning
    perspective
❑ Bravery
❑ Perseverance
❑ Honesty

❑ Zest
❑ Love
❑ Kindness
❑ Empathy
❑ Compassion
❑ Sense of humor
❑ Spirituality
❑ Pastoral counseling
❑ Spiritual direction
    & guidance
❑ Fishing and outdoors
❑ Sciences
❑ Graphic design
❑ Liturgical service
❑ Learning

2. Now, ask a family member or a friend to give you feedback about what they think your strengths are. List 3 of those strengths here.

Strength 1: _____

Strength 2: _____

Strength 3:_____

3. Now that you have the Checklist completed and input from your family or friends, narrow down the list into your **TOP 5 Strengths**.

Strength 1: _____

Strength 2: _____

Strength 3:_____

Strength 4: _____

Strength 5: _____

USING YOUR STRENGTHS TO SERVE THE CHURCH

Now that you have identified some of your strengths, turn your focus back to discernment. We have already established the fact that the Church needs all different kinds of men, each with their own set of strengths, to serve as priests. The Church has many needs and serves diverse people. A priesthood with many different kinds of strengths helps to address all the needs of the people. The Catholic Church has already started to put this into practice. Some dioceses are asking priests what their strengths are and basing decisions about their ministerial assignments on their strengths. Fr. Adam Verona of the Pittsburgh Diocese underwent a strength-based assessment in 2017 and was quoted in the local Catholic newspaper:

"[What] I experienced was that Bishop David Zubik and his staff want to see every priest flourish. They are very interested in what we want to do in our ministry and in what we see ourselves as good at doing. Everybody has different gifts and talents. We cannot all be everything for everyone. I tried to do that as a priest, but you can't. We all have to look at what each priest can contribute in each role."

Your personal strengths are something that you bring to your vocation. No matter what vocation God is calling you to, those strengths are going to be there with you. Imagine how you can use your strengths in the priesthood. By focusing on strengths, you can turn your fears about what you cannot do into feelings of excitement and curiosity about what you can do to put your strengths into practice to serve people. We have encouraged you to take an active approach to discerning the priesthood throughout this book. We want you to get involved, motivated, and to take simple steps to discover God's will in your life. One of the ways to embrace simple and active discernment is to start using your strengths to serve God and the Church.

Using your strengths to discern God's will is fairly straightforward. Pick a strength and figure out how you can use it to enrich your faith life. If you are a person who is good at giving speeches, volunteer to give a talk to your youth group. If you have a knack for leadership, consider being a small group leader at a retreat. If you have the strength of humor, bring your humor to the soup kitchen and brighten the place up. If you are a skilled musician, take your talent to the local nursing home and put on a performance. There are many different ways to use your strengths to discern God's will in your life.

4. What are three ways you can use your strengths to serve the Church?

    _____

    _____

    _____

5. Now that you have identified your strengths and figured out ways to use them, it's time to get active. Your homework is to use your strengths to serve the Church!

Write down your plan on how to use at least one of your strengths this week.

STRENGTH	DAY	STRENGTH PUT INTO PRACTICE
Example: Singing	Thursday	Join the choir practice at my parish

SIMPLE AND ACTIVE

1. Use the lists provided in the chapter to identify your personal strengths.

   ☦ Ask family members, friends, teachers, or coaches for their input.

   ☦ Consider how your strengths could make you a good priest.

2. Think of three ways you can use your strengths to serve the Church.

   ✟ Be creative about how your strengths can help to serve other people.

   ✟ Use your strengths in youth groups, discernment groups, soup kitchens, nursing homes, and other places where you can minister to people in need.

   ✟ Ask others how you might use your strengths to serve the Church.

CHAPTER 10

G O I N G   A L L   I N

KEEP IT SIMPLE

Listening for your call from God is not easy. You are likely to become confused while you listen. Questions naturally arise: What does God want me to do? Does he really want me to become a priest? Who should I talk to you? What should I do? We promised to simplify your discernment with this book. In each chapter, we identified a common barrier among men and how to overcome that barrier simply. If you think God might be calling you to consider the priesthood, but are confused and questioning, you can focus on this one point. If the idea of the priesthood has come up repeatedly in your life, then you need to do something about it. The repeated frequency of God's voice is a tell-tale sign that God wants you to take action on the idea of the priesthood.

If this is true for you, welcomed or unwelcomed, then now is the time to act. You are worthy of laying it all out on the line and finding an answer from God. It is risky to go all in and you might fear the uncertainty of the next steps. However, discovering your vocation is worthy of the risk. The alternative is going the rest of your life without ever really knowing what God wants from you. We are afraid that you might miss out on what God wants you to do with your life if you do not keep it simple, recognize God's repeated calls to you, and then act.

ALL-IN ACTION

The main character has to make a major decision in any really good movie. They choose whether or not to take action. They choose whether or not to go *All In*. Of course, we always want the main character to go all in. We cheer when the character takes decisive action. The drama begins to unfold and we are drawn further into the plot and wonder how is this story is going to end. A couple of particular scenes come to mind:

- ✞ At the end of *Lord of the Rings: Return of the King*, Aragorn finds himself and his small army surrounded by a much bigger army. However, he knows that Frodo is still out there, in need of help. Rather than surrender, Aragorn looks around, says "For Frodo" and leads a straight-on charge!

- ✞ In *Creed*, Adonis Creed is living a plush life in California in the business world while boxing in taverns on the weekends. He decides that if he wants to be a boxer, he has to move to Philadelphia, and train 100% of the time. No more moonlighting on weekends, he has to go all in. He shows up at the gym day after day until Rocky agrees to train him.

We do not think that any movie critic or professor of cinema has drawn parallels between Aragorn in *Lord of the Rings* and Adonis Creed from *Creed*, but allow us to do just that. We were introduced to both Adonis and Aragorn hanging out in dark and shady taverns, they both had royal bloodlines initially unknown to the general public, and they went through a prolonged period of change. They both made the decision to go all in—laying everything on the line for the sake of their mission. Adonis and Aragorn's willingness to go all in enabled them to fulfill their purpose and find greatness. Aragorn became a king and Adonis a boxing champion. They were men who had been changed for the better over an extended period of time. In many ways, those movie scenes and characters served as an inspiration for the title of this book.

Men who are discerning the priesthood reach a point in their story when they have to go all in. The decision to go all in is not impulsive and fleeting. Rather, the decision to go all in is deliberate, courageous, and requires commitment and responsibility. An all-in decision is made after careful analysis, identification of the goal, and a determined focus to work toward the goal. You have heard God's repeated call to consider the priesthood. Next, you have to repeatedly engage in the deliberate actions to find out if God is really *calling* you to the priesthood.

God wants you to find your calling. Your calling will not remain hidden forever; some work and commitment is required. As Rocky tells Adonis while training—it's "one step at time, one punch at a time, one round at time." Add it all up, and you have gone all in. Rocky actually gave advice based on scripture, as Ecclesiastes 9:10 says, "Whatever the activity in which you engage, do it with all of your ability." You are worthy of the risk, challenge, and commitment that goes into discovering and living out God's calling for you. We implore you to make the big decision to pursue the priesthood actively. Jump into the swimming pool as Archbishop Listecki proclaimed! Follow up that big decision to go all in with all of the other actions that will support your vocational discernment such as visiting the seminary, talking to the vocations director, and going on a retreat. You can become the hero of your discernment story by going all in.

OVERCOME THE PSYCHOLOGICAL BARRIERS

There is an old saying among marathon runners that you are not ready to run your next marathon until you have forgotten about the pain and agony of your last marathon. Running a marathon entails countless hours of training, battling fatigue, and overcoming the inner voice that says, "I can't run anymore," only to keep running. Figuring what God wants you to do with your life requires the same persistence and the ability to overcome adversity.

In Chapters 3–8, we challenged you to overcome psychological barriers such as perpetual discernment and uncertainty. We directed you to surround yourself with people who are going to encourage your vocation and to take on the discouragers. We asked you to think about what kind of Catholic man you are and how you can be a better man. We prompted you to identify your strengths and put them into action in the service of the Church. We do not want you to be held back by the many barriers that men face. You can overcome perpetual discernment, uncertainty, fears about celibacy, and discouragers. You can put your strengths to use by serving others and learning from your experiences.

Following God's plan is a lot like athletic training as St. Paul told the Corinthians (9:24-27): "Run in such a way as to get the prize. Everyone who competes in the games goes into strict training. They do it to get a crown that will not last, but we do it to get a crown that will last forever. Therefore, I do not run like a man running aimlessly; I do not fight like a man beating the air. No, I challenge my body so I will not be disqualified from the prize."

We laid out a plan for your discernment that provides you with the active training to overcome barriers. The simple and active plan gives you direction and focus so you do not run aimlessly any longer. Yes, the active steps will challenge you, but the prize of finding and living your vocation is there for your taking. Rather than run away from God, it is time for you to run toward God. When you run toward God, you are looking forward, ahead, and into the future. If you take on the challenge of going all in on your vocation, you can look forward to the meaning and purpose that comes with fulfilling God's will in your life.

A FULFILLING LIFE

In 2011, priest-psychologist Fr. Stephen Rossetti published *Why Priests are Happy: A Study of the Psychological and Spiritual Health of Priest.* Fr. Rossetti surveyed 2,482 priests from twenty-nine dioceses in the United States. Fr. Rossetti's study concluded that there are "extraordinarily high rates of priestly happiness and satisfaction." Priests tend to like the priesthood and find satisfaction in their vocational calling. In fact, their satisfaction rates were among the highest observed when compared to any profession, vocation, or career in the United States. In other words, priests consider their vocation more fulfilling than most everyone else.

Perhaps men are observing priests living a fulfilling life and want to do likewise. Georgetown University's Center for Applied Research in the Apostolate (CARA) has been tracking the number of seminarians in the United States since 1965. The lowest number of seminarians was in 1995—3,172. Since then, the numbers have been slowly increasing to 3,520 in 2016, which is the highest total since 1995. There are also fascinating case studies of some dioceses that are seeing an increase in the number of men studying to be priests. For example, the dioceses of Cleveland in Ohio and Madison in Wisconsin are gaining national attention for not only the increased number of men studying to be priests but the support given to those men such as scholarships and encouragement from people in the pews.

Dioceses are starting to realize that it is not enough simply to "pray for vocations to the priesthood" but to provide financial support for the cost of priest school (otherwise known as formation in the seminary). Similarly, dioceses are allocating more personnel resources to mentor and train men such as full-time vocation directors and staff. There is no silver bullet, but more dioceses are realizing that it takes many initiatives to increase the number of men who become priests.

Similarly, a deeper look at the psychological research related to priests paints a different picture than the prevailing public stereotypes.

- ✝ 3–6% of all Catholic priests were alleged to have committed child sexual abuse between 1950–2002, which is a lower prevalence rate than the general population of men. In other words, the vast majority of Catholic priests are not pedophiles.
- ✝ In two studies (Plante, 2005; Isacco et al., 2017) over a ten-year period, men who entered the seminary were, by and large, found to have few psychological concerns and were not psychologically dysfunctional.

Although we cannot promise you a perfectly happy, healthy, and fulfilling life as a priest, the studies speak volumes. We know that the priests in Father Rossetti's study went all in on their vocational discernment. They conquered the many barriers they faced and relentlessly pursued God's will. They did not fall victim to perpetual discernment. They heard God's call and took action. They gained the courage to enter the seminary. While in the seminary, they transformed themselves into better men with the guidance of the Church. They dealt with discouragers, questions about celibacy, and unworthiness. After years of preparation, they were presented to the Church community as worthy of the priesthood on the day of their ordination. And now we know that most of them are living meaningful, fulfilling, and happy lives. These

men were ordained to the priesthood and provide real life examples of what it means to go all in. They are living proof that
going all in on your vocation leads to a life of fulfillment. If
they can do it, so can you.

ABOUT THE
AUTHORS

ANTHONY ISACCO, PHD, is associate professor in the graduate psychology programs at Chatham University and Owner of Puritan Psychological Services. He is a nationally recognized expert on Catholic seminarian, deacon, and priest mental health. He resides in Pittsburgh with his wife, Celeste, and their four daughters.

DOMENICK TIRABASSI, MS, a professional counselor and speaker, is a doctoral student in clinical psychology at Wisconsin School of Professional Psychology. He has published and presented empirical research aimed at enhancing the psychological wellbeing of priests and seminarians. He lives in Milwaukee with his wife, Christi, and their daughter.